East Devon Pebblebed Heaths

240 million years in the making

East Devon Pebblebed Heaths

240 million years in the making

by Andrew Cooper

Pebblebed Heaths
CONSERVATION TRUST

First Published 2007
By East Devon Pebblebed Heaths Conservation Trust
Rolle Estate Office
East Budleigh
Budleigh Salterton
Devon
EX9 7DP
Charity Reg No: 1109514

and Impress Books Ltd
Innovation Centre, Rennes Drive,
University of Exeter Campus, Exeter EX4 4RN

Designed and artworked by Chalk and Ward Advertising, Exeter, Devon

Printed and bound in England by Butler and Tanner, Frome, Somerset

British Library Cataloguing in Publication Data

A catalogue record for this book is available from the British Library

ISBN 978-0-9556239-0-5

This book is dedicated to all the generations of mankind who, through their toil and endeavour, have made the Pebblebed Heaths what they are today, and also to future generations, to whom the responsibility of stewardship now passes.

contents

AYLESBEARE
COMMON

HARPFORD
COMMON

HAWKERLAND

MUTTERS MOOR

COLATON RALEIGH
COMMON

WOODBURY
COMMON

BICTON COMMON

EAST BUDLEIGH
COMMON

DALDITCH
COMMON

foreword
by 22nd Baron Clinton

Over 240 million years of history, the beautiful landscape of the East Devon Pebblebed Heaths.

I am delighted to write the foreword to this unique and very special book. The seven Commons and Mutters Moor, which have been owned by the Estate from the 17th century and now form the majority of the East Devon Pebblebed Heaths, have always played a central role in our stewardship of the East Devon Estate.

Andrew Cooper reminds us how relatively insignificant mankind is in relation to the remarkable changes that have occurred to this unique geology and landscape. Over 240 million years of history, mankind's stewardship of the Pebblebed Heaths covers only a few thousand years. Estate archives contain many letters and documents which demonstrate the importance of the heaths to those who earned a living from them. Today the heaths are valued for different reasons. A clear theme emerges and that is of change. As the geology, landscape and habitat has evolved over millions of years, so mankind's use of heathland has changed in just a few hundred.

The publication of this book marks the formation of the East Devon Pebblebed Heaths Conservation Trust, a charity set up to manage the heaths for the public benefit. This is an important milestone and one which reflects a new set of agendas to be 'balanced': public access and recreation, nature conservation, military training and forestry. I believe that all these agendas can be accommodated with effective dialogue, education and pragmatism. The Trust, and this book, have a major part to play in communicating the 'story' of the heaths; past, present and also future. The debate about the impact of climate change adds a new dimension and urgency to the story about the future.

Andrew Cooper's book, commissioned by the Trust, is timely and will hopefully be read by a wide audience, featuring on the bookshelves and coffee tables of not just those living locally to the heaths but also all those with an interest and passion in the stewardship of this special place for the benefit of future generations.

introduction

The result of a fascinating story of
dinosaurs, geology, social history and
wildlife management.

Imagine a land at the dawn of the age of dinosaurs, a place where some of the world's first giant reptiles once roamed. A hot dry landscape littered with boulders and smaller rounded rocks. These stones were shaped by their journey over hundreds of miles, worn smooth in the turbulence of a great river and flash floods generated by torrential storms. At first sight the ribbons of green vegetation flanking the river's course across the desert and a few large crocodile-like creatures appear to be the only life.

Dinosaurs eventually inhabited the earth for over a hundred million years, before their sudden decline. Over time the rocks upon which they hatched and hunted, foraged and fought, became just another layer, drowned by tropical seas or lifted high by immense volcanic forces and eroded again. Slowly the original great continent upon which they lived began to divide and drift north, away from the equator and blazing sun, carrying the land that would one day become southern England. After freezing and thawing during successive Ice Ages, Britain finally became an island covered by a vast impenetrable forest. Indeed, so extensive was the woodland that only mountain tops and wetlands remained bare of trees. Even nomadic human hunters probably feared to tread in this ancient wildwood where wolves and bears hunted for food, wild boar ploughed the floor and ferocious giant cattle browsed on leaves. This was no place for people. Then the first farmers began clearing the wood with stone axes and fire to leave a grassy wilderness in their wake. Once a dark and threatening place shaded by towering trees, the open rolling landscape now had views to the sea. In time the land became a heathland with heathers and other wild flowers, rich in nature and the history of people's lives.

This is a story that has taken millions of years in the making, a tale of myths and monsters, real people and important events in a landscape scarred by preparations for war and peace. Today it is part of a great estate, a place like no other on earth – the remarkable East Devon Pebblebed Heaths.

chapter 1

the past

rolling stones

As you walk along the beach at Budleigh Salterton, the smooth, rounded stones beneath your feet are intriguing and have an amazing story to tell. Unlike any other rock found in southern England they form part of a large pebblebed stretching over 40 miles inland as far as the Somerset border, in places over 32 metres deep. Along the Devon and Dorset coast they can be found on several beaches and even out to sea, down to 40 metres deep. In recent years the mystery of these stones was finally solved. The East Devon pebbles have come a long way, both in time and space.

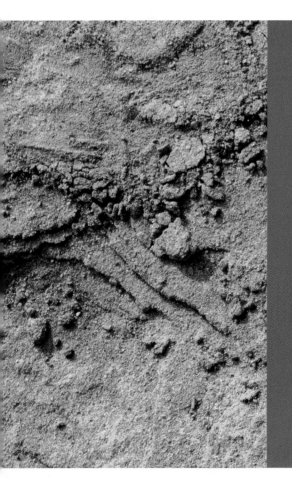

East Devon's dramatic red Triassic sandstone.

famous rocks

Devon is famed worldwide for having lent its name to an entire period in geological time. The sands and stones of Devon make it geologically one of the most diverse counties in England. The landscape spans some 400 million years and includes rocks that belong to the Devonian, Carboniferous, Permian, Triassic, Jurassic, Cretaceous, Tertiary and Quaternary periods. Devon has seen great changes from mainly marine in the Devonian and Carboniferous, arid deserts during the Permian and Triassic, and the return of marine conditions in the Jurassic and Cretaceous, with the retreat of seas through the Tertiary to the present day.

Mountain-building towards the end of the Carboniferous further complicated the picture. This caused uplifting of the Devonian and Carboniferous rocks leading to extensive folding and faulting together with the deep intrusion of granite to form Dartmoor, one of the largest and most southerly upland areas in England.

This diverse geological history has produced a wonderfully varied landscape. The red Triassic sandstone, dramatic mudstone cliffs and the colourful pebblebeds around Budleigh Salterton create one of the county's most remarkable features.

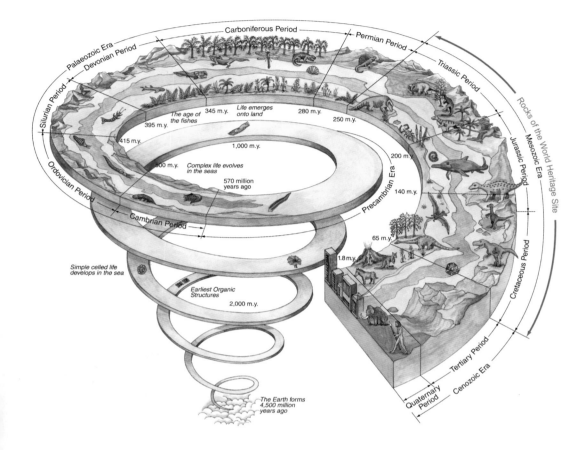

Labels on illustration:

Carboniferous Period
Permian Period
Palaeozoic Era
Devonian Period
Triassic Period
Silurian Period
345 m.y. — Life emerges onto land
395 m.y. — The age of the fishes
280 m.y.
250 m.y.
415 m.y.
1,000 m.y.
Ordovician Period
500 m.y. — Complex life evolves in the seas
570 million years ago
200 m.y.
Cambrian Period
140 m.y.
Precambrian Era
Simple celled life develops in the sea
65 m.y.
Earliest Organic Structures
2,000 m.y.
1.8 m.y.
The Earth forms 4,500 million years ago
Rocks of the World Heritage Site
Mesozoic Era
Jurassic Period
Cretaceous Period
Tertiary Period
Cenozoic Era
Quaternary Period

Long before dinosaurs lived on the earth during the Mesozoic era some 225 million years ago, a giant raging river carried hard pebbles across a desert. That river deposited the stones in a deep bed that now extends across part of East Devon. The origin of the rock is sandstone cemented by silica under great pressure to form a very hard stone. Identical quartzite rocks formed some 440 million years ago are today found across the English Channel in Brittany. They also contain the same fossils, mostly marine shellfish called Brachiopods. These rocks originally date back to the Ordovician and Silurian periods of geological time and belong to an important stage in the formation of our planet.

Around 350 million years ago the rocks from which the pebbles came were caught up in an event of global proportions. All the land masses at that time came together to form a single giant super-continent called Gondwana or Pangaea. The resulting collision of continents threw up a chain of mountains stretching from present day Spain through France, south-west England and on into Ireland. Molten rock was also injected deep into the deforming crust and there it solidified as granite. The land that would one day become the British Isles then lay at the centre of a vast single continent. North and South America lay to the west and the European continent to the south, east and north. The red colour of the rocks tells us that it was a hot dry desert, not unlike parts of Australia and African Namib of today, or perhaps even the surface of the planet Mars. That red colouration is caused by iron which is a common metal in the Earth's crust. Normally iron combines with organic material to form other compounds. In a desert organic material is scarce and the iron becomes part of the sediment where it oxidises to produce its distinctive rusty red colour.

By the early Triassic period, between 250–230 million years ago, the climate changed dramatically. It became much wetter. Heavy rains in the Armorican Mountains to the south formed a huge branching river flooding north, rather like the Nile winding through the African Sahara desert today. As the quartzite rocks were slowly weathered out of the mountain sides they were tumbled along the river beds by the torrent. Bashed and buffeted against each other they eventually became rounded into pebbles. The scale must have been breathtaking in its extent, a deep and violent flow of silt-laden water. Today its pebbles are found all the way up the Severn Valley and as far as Cheshire. So the pebbles on the East Devon Pebblebed Heaths are probably around 240 million years old.

profile of a pebble

Sandstone forms from wind- or water-deposited layers of sand. Some of the resulting stone is soft and easily carved, while others are surprisingly hard. The East Devon pebbles are hard, typically rounded and often very smooth. They are not spherical but more flattened in shape. However, the larger pebbles up to 20 cm in size are usually more rounded. They are also banded. These bands are the original layers of sand. Some pebbles are blotchy in appearance or mottled red or brown in colour. Looking closely, small hollow spaces mark the presence of fossil creatures, usually ancient marine bi-valve shellfish, related to modern day razor shells and cockles. The strength of the rock comes from the fact that the gaps between the sand grains have been filled with silica – a natural cement.

The famous Budleigh Salterton pebblebeds can best be seen in the cliffs on the western side of the town. Offshore they even form an underwater ledge marked by a cluster of lobster pots, while inland they can be found on the high ground of Woodbury Common between Budleigh and Exmouth.

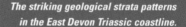

While that ancient mountain chain has now all but gone, worn down over eons of time, evidence of the monumental forces that created the great Armorican Mountains can still be seen in the zig-zag folding of the rocks at places such as Hartland Quay in north Devon. Today only the eroded granite stumps remain to shape our present landscapes – the moors and tors, granite cliffs and outcrops of Cornwall, Devon and Brittany in France.

The Budleigh pebbles are like no other rock on this coast. Perhaps not surprising, considering their long journey back in Triassic times. For thousands of years the pebbles fell onto the beaches and carried by waves, spread along the coast. Because they are so different from the local rocks, they are easy to spot. Budleigh pebbles are found all along Chesil Beach to Portland and beyond. Some can even be recognised at Hurst Spit and on the shores of the Solent and even Hastings in Kent. The pebbles provide real evidence of long shore drift, the movement of beach material due to wave action. Since the last Ice Age, the dominant wave direction in the English Channel is from the Atlantic travelling east. So waves tend to strike the beach at an angle, moving eastwards. As a result, they push sand and pebbles in that direction. But their progress is not direct: they zig-zag along the beach, pushed eastwards by the incoming wave and then dragged down the beach as each wave drains away. Weaker waves formed by winds blowing down the Channel are thought to transport some pebbles back towards the west but they have not travelled anything like as far. Some East Devon pebbles are also to be found as far west as Slapton. The shape of our shore has changed considerably over time with the waxing and waning of the Ice Ages and corresponding changes in sea levels. It is also thought that the prevailing winds came from the east during the glacial periods. Perhaps more revealing are the pebbles that can be seen embedded in ancient raised beaches, 12–15 metres high in the cliffs. This is tangible proof of changes in sea level over 100,000 years ago. And if you want to experience the view from that ancient level, just take a trip on a train, between Dawlish and Teignmouth. The track is actually built on the raised beach.

While the majority of the East Devon Triassic rocks were deposited in rivers, others were not. The striking patterns visible in the rocks at Orcombe Point and Straight Point may be the remains of sand dunes that were blown through the

real rolling stones

Sometimes the most unlikely event brings a smile to a geologist's face. One such occasion was the need for a hard platform to help with the drilling of a bore hole on Budleigh Salterton beach. The dumping of two truck loads of fresh red pebbles in 1992 provided an interesting opportunity to watch the subsequent progress of the stones along the coast. Scattered by spring tides and washed by waves the dispersal of the pebbles took everyone by surprise. In just ten years the stones travelled over five miles and they are still on the move!

ancient desert. Wind-shaped pebbles known as 'drycanters' (or 'dreikanter,' literally 'three-faced') can also be found at Budleigh Salterton. These pebbles have been sand-blasted. They have a flat base with triangular sides etched and sculpted by primeval sand-laden winds.

Otter Sandstone deposited in rivers lies above the pebblebeds and can be seen around the mouth of the River Otter, along to Ladram Bay and as far as Jacob's Ladder near Sidmouth. Above the pebblebeds, Mercia Mudstone settled in huge temporary lakes that flooded the vast desert basin from time to time.

the jurassic coast

Take a walk along the coast and let your imagination run riot as you travel back in time. Indeed so rich are these parts in rocks and fossils, they have been described as a geologist's dream. No wonder that the cliffs and beaches of Lyme Bay are part of England's first natural World Heritage Site. Yet what makes this coast so remarkable is that the cliffs here record 185 million years of earth history in just 95 miles of coastline.

The key to its exceptional status is a twist of fate, or more precisely the tilting of rocks that lie between Exmouth in East Devon and Studland in Dorset. Here, the layers of rocks mainly tilt gently to the east. This means that the oldest rocks form the cliffs in the west and progressively younger rocks 'dip down' to form the cliffs to the east. The red rocks of East Devon were formed some 250 million years ago in the Triassic period when vast deserts covered the area. The dark clay rocks of West Dorset formed in a tropical sea around 200 million years ago. They are the earliest Jurassic rocks. Towards the end of this period, the sea levels dropped and forests grew fringed with swamps and lagoons across which herds of dinosaurs roamed. 100 million years ago the sea levels rose again, flooding the area under a vast sea in which fine white chalk formed from the shells of millions of minute marine creatures.

Throughout this time life flourished and the evidence can be found in the form of fantastic fossils. The huge variety of rock types has formed many different and superb coastal features creating spectacular scenery of beaches, bays, landslides, headlands and wave-sculpted sea stacks.

a natural history

The extraordinary story of the East Devon Pebblebeds begins over 240 million years ago. The Permian period which had lasted for around 42 million years, came to an abrupt and terrible end. It was an event of global catastrophic proportions. The cause is still not fully understood but the resulting devastation killed 95% of all life in the oceans and 70% of all land plant and animal families. It was a pivotal point for life on earth. At that time the climate was dry and desert covered most of the land. Violent storms washed down large amounts of sediment from mountains. Flash floods turned dry river beds into raging torrents surging through the surrounding parched valleys and desert plains.

Dry river beds similar to those left by flash floods at the end of the Permian period.

the greatest extinction of all time

Life flourished almost unchallenged during the Carboniferous and Permian periods between 354 and 248 million years ago. Crinoids and corals, nautilus-like creatures and ammonoids, as well as fishes, all thrived in the sea. Amphibians and mammal-like reptiles continued to invade the land. But after more than 100 million years of relative stability, the end of the Permian period was marked by an event far worse than the one that caused the demise of the dinosaur. The Permian came to an abrupt finish, marked by the biggest mass extinction our planet has ever seen. This is the nearest that life on Earth has yet come to total annihilation.

In the sea, entire reefs were destroyed, and with them went many corals as well as major groups of other animals. Sea life underwent huge change, opening the way for new groups of corals and previously minor groups of marine creatures to expand. On land the end of the Permian mass extinction destroyed entire communities of amphibians and mammal-like reptiles, leaving only a few behind from which the dinosaurs, pterosaurs, marine reptiles and mammals arose.

The scale of the event can be seen in fossil records where whole habitats vanished, taking millions of years to return. It is not just geologists who know this. There is a famous 'coal gap' after this mass extinction, where miners find no coal in the subsequent layers of rock. Entire forests were so completely destroyed that the burial of rotting plant material in significant amounts ended for some 20 million years. This marked the start of the Triassic and a new chapter in life on Earth.

The Permian extinction left a wilderness. Where life once prospered, the single large continent of Pangaea was now eerily bleak and empty. For the first few million years of the next great geological period of the Triassic, plants that had survived the devastation formed scrub vegetation along rivers and streams. During the Triassic the area that is now Devon was a very different place to the green and pleasant land of today. Scorched by a subtropical sun, mountains up to 3,000m dominated the distant skyline. The dry conditions that began during the Permian period continued through much of the Triassic. This was a harsh time for life to survive, yet it did and eventually began to thrive. Despite the terrible conditions the seasonal rivers allowed plants and animals to live along their banks. Primitive vegetation grew in green ribbons running through the desert and creatures sought the shade beneath towering primitive conifers, tree ferns, horsetails and cycads. The extinction had cleared the stage for surviving reptiles to evolve and take over. The Triassic was once considered to be the dawn of the dinosaurs but it was much more than that. It was a wild and wonderful world where all kinds of strange animals lived and died. But none were true dinosaurs, just the supporting cast. The domination of dinosaurs would not begin for another 50 million years. In the meantime the Triassic was a world of truly fantastic creatures that set terrestrial life on the path to the present day.

Two major groups of reptiles were poised to dominate life on earth in the future. The Synapsids were the first to gain prominence and would eventually give rise to mammals. It was, however, the Diapsids that would soon be ruling the earth, paving the way for dinosaurs. By the end of this period many of our present groups of reptiles and amphibians would be represented, including frogs, turtles and crocodiles. The first true mammals also appeared at this time. We know this from fossils found in Triassic rocks, although such finds are rare and often poorly preserved. Occasionally a fossil is discovered almost intact. One such creature was found near Sidmouth. It was a mammal-like reptile called *rhynchosaurus*. The remains were in such a fine state of preservation that an impressive reconstruction of the animal was possible. So far evidence of ten species of reptiles, amphibians and fish have been found on the East Devon coast. This represents the richest site of its time in Britain, helping us paint an amazing picture of Mid-Triassic life.

	Main rock strata (simplified)	Location
CRETACEOUS PERIOD (65 million years old)	CHALK	Beer, Axmouth to Lyme Regis, White Nothe, Lulworth, Old Harry Rocks
	UPPER GREENSAND	Widespread throughout the Site
	GAULT	
	LOWER GREENSAND	North-east of Swanage
	WEALDEN GROUP	Lulworth, Swanage
JURASSIC PERIOD (140 million years old)	PURBECK GROUP	Portland(in part), Lulworth, Durlston Bay
	PORTLAND GROUP	Portland, Lulworth, Durlston Bay
	KIMMERIDGE CLAY FORMATION	Kimmeridge Bay, Portland, Portland Harbour shore, The Fleet
	CORALLIAN GROUP	Wyke Regis, Osmington Mills, The Fleet, Portland Harbour shore
	OXFORD CLAY	East of Weymouth, Chickerell
	MIDDLE JURASSIC	West Bay to The Fleet shore
	LIAS GROUP	West of Lyme Regis to Burton Bradstock
TRIASSIC PERIOD (200 million years old)	PENARTH GROUP	East of Axmouth
	MERCIA MUDSTONE GROUP	West of Sidmouth to Branscombe, Seaton to east of Axmouth
	OTTER SANDSTONE FORMATION	Budleigh Salterton to Sidmouth
	BUDLEIGH SALTERTON PEBBLE BEDS	Budleigh Salterton
	AYLESBEARE MUDSTONE GROUP	Exmouth to Budleigh Salterton

250 million years old

The impression this conjures is of a weird and wonderful landscape. Sunrise over a red desert reveals a network of rivers transporting the pebblebeds of East Devon from their mountain bedrock. The air is mercifully cool at this hour in the desert. The rains that fed the mountain deluge are beginning to vanish once more. Now, only a gentle flowing stream meanders through water-worn stones. Along the banks tall monkey puzzle-like conifers and ginkgo trees shade the ground where tree-ferns thrive. In the river's muddy margins Horsetail plants grow in thick beds. Huge crocodile-like amphibians lurk in lazy pools and large lizards bask on boulders, warming in the early morning sun. Suddenly they are disturbed by the arrival of several much bigger kin. Rhynchosaurs, with their strange rodent-like jaws, push through the riverside undergrowth, scattering monster-sized scorpions in their path.

A reconstruction of Mid-Triassic times in Devon based on specimens found within the East Devon Otter Sandstone.

Illustration courtesy of Professor Mike Benton, University of Bristol.

The discovery of the remains of a large reptile near Ladram Bay sent ripples of excitement through scientific circles and fired the imagination of local people. In the spring of 1990 geologists from Bristol and Plymouth Universities added a new chapter to their understanding of a remarkable period in time. The Otter Sandstones of East Devon have previously yielded important evidence of Mid-Triassic life over 235 million year ago. While the assorted fossilised bones of fish, amphibians and some reptiles have also been identified, the unearthing of the most complete skeleton of a rhynchosaur (which lived 240 million years ago) yet uncovered in Devon was sensational news. This reptile belongs to an impressive group of prehistoric creatures known as archosauromorphs, closely related to the archosaurs, the group that eventually gave rise to all dinosaurs, birds, crocodiles and even formidable winged pterosaurs.

Since the 1830s the remains of long-extinct creatures from the dawn of the age of dinosaurs have been found elsewhere in Britain and Europe, but it was not until the 1980s that the significance of the East Devon coast was fully realised. The richness of the fossil beds in the region is now renowned worldwide.

To fully appreciate the scale and character of a rhynchosaur, an impressive life-size model of the creature has been commissioned by the East Devon Pebblebed Heaths Conservation Trust and Clinton Devon Estates, and is destined for public display in the Royal Albert Memorial Museum, Exeter. The purpose of the remarkable beak-like structure of its upper jaw is perhaps its most intriguing feature. The living landscape of the Triassic is now dead and long since buried beneath layers of later sediments upon which dinosaurs once hunted and grazed. The pebblebeds of East Devon were to lie largely hidden for a further 240 million years.

ice ages

Over the last two million years the climate of Britain has varied widely from extreme arctic to subtropical conditions. As temperatures rose and fell the arctic ice cap expanded and contracted again. Each Ice Age lasted around 100,000 years and the intervening periods of warmth just a tenth of that time. Although up to 50 cold and 50 warm periods are known, only four were thought to be severe enough for massive ice sheets to extend across most of the British Isles. The intervening warm periods were hotter than today. During less cold glacial times the ice covered the uplands during winter, only occasionally extending to lower levels. The legacy of the Ice Ages can still be seen all around us, as they largely created the landscape we see today.

In places the great ice sheets rose over two kilometres high, crushing all life below. Fortunately the south-west of England did not experience the full weight of the advancing ice, as their southward movement did not extend this far. But Devon did not escape unscathed. Far offshore the sea surface froze as pack ice formed in winter. At its worst, Devon was in the grip of an arctic climate. Here, tundra vegetation struggled to survive. Blanketed by deep snow in winter, permafrost lay not far underground, even during summer. Consequently water could not drain away and so just flowed across the surface, forming seasonal streams of melted water.

Repeated freezing and thawing eventually shatters exposed rocks and the resulting rubble mix pours down every slope, smoothing sharp edges and covering cliffs. As the ice sheets melted and grew again, so sea levels worldwide rose and fell. Some shorelines can still be found above the present day sea levels. Raised beaches are a feature of Devon's coastline, especially in the south-east of the county.

Bering Glacier, Alaska: landscape similar to that of the Ice Ages, the legacy of which can be seen today.

Image courtesy of Ronald Bruhn, University of Utah.

climate

The south coast of Devon enjoys one of the mildest climates in Britain. Bathed in warm prevailing winds from across the Atlantic and ocean currents generated by the tropical Gulf Stream, the region is blessed with a plentiful supply of rain. Most of the moisture falls in the west and on the highest ground. While parts of Dartmoor can account for over 2.3 metres, much of East Devon receives less than 800 mm of rain a year. On the coast frosts are rare but Dartmoor has snow most winters. Generally the south-west of England, being a peninsula, does not have such extremes of temperatures as further north and east of Britain. In Devon, summers are seldom too hot and winters rarely very cold, while the sunshine record is especially high around Lyme Bay.

Melting ice is a powerful agent of erosion. Many pebbles must have seen their first light of day since Triassic times after being torn from their beds by glacial river torrents. When the ice caps finally disappeared, the southern edge of ice retreated north, the ground thawed and life slowly recovered again. Plants began to grow. Woodland soon spread across the landscape. Apart from wetlands and mountain tops trees dominated the scene. Animals arrived from southern Europe to exploit the new food source. People followed in their wake, returning to areas that human hunters had occupied before the last expansion of ice. There was plenty to hunt and places to shelter. The first trees to establish themselves were birch and pine, and the first animals, reindeer, wolf, arctic fox, horse and bear.

At the end of the last Ice Age, around 11,000 years ago the sea level was so low that early nomadic hunters could have walked from Spain to south-west England. Since then rising sea levels drowned many rivers and formed estuaries in the coastal valleys of Devon. The climate continued to warm. Along the south coast, rivers continued to deposit silt and clay, while peat accumulated in the lower reaches. Where arctic tundra gave way to forests of birch and pine, dense deciduous woods soon began to grow. Today the fossil remains of forests, drowned by rising seas and covered by sand, are sometimes exposed after storms and spring tides. In time, oak and hazel came to dominate the woods of western England and during summer, six thousand years ago, the pebblebeds of East Devon would have darkened in their shade.

On the well-drained heights above Woodbury, early farmers began clearing that ancient wildwood, first with flint axes then later with the cutting edge of bronze. These people opened the way for the formation of heath. The disappearance of tree cover brought in a new wave of wild plants and animals more suited to life on open grasslands.

Down on the coast the rising sea cut into soft cliffs releasing yet more pebbles. Offshore huge quantities lay submerged. Over the last few millennia the increasing sea level, combined with movement of tides and winter gales, carried many of the stones along the shore. By Tudor times, despite the efforts of local people and Henry VIII's advisors, a growing pebble bank prevented larger ships from trading with the port of Axmouth.

Even today fresh pebbles are still being revealed, exposed by wind and waves on the coast and heavy rain inland. So the next time you pick up a pebble in East Devon, remember it is not just any old stone. You may wonder in awe at the lost world it represents, resting in the palm of your hand and its journey through time and the incredible story it tells.

A Bronze Age axehead found by Roger Stokes at Rushmore Farm below Woodbury Castle in 1960.

Image courtesy of Roger Stokes.

an impressive heritage

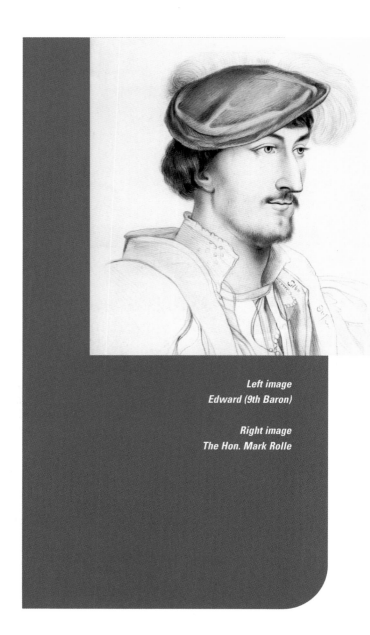

Left image
Edward (9th Baron)

Right image
The Hon. Mark Rolle

The East Devon Pebblebed Heaths are inextricably linked to the Clinton and Rolle families. By any standards the Clinton history is impressive. A family of great antiquity with a distinguished and complex lineage, they played an important part in English life as both warriors and statesmen. Nearly eight hundred years ago during the reign of Henry I between 1100 and 1135, Geoffrey de Clinton was a powerful man. As Lord Chamberlain to the King he was Treasurer and Chief Justice of England. Few other families can claim ancestors that were ennobled by Plantagenet kings, or ranked so prominently before the time of the Crusades.

The Barony of Clinton was created after John de Clinton's victory in 1298 over the Scots at Falkirk. Nearly 250 years later the family link to Devon was established in 1550 with the acquisition of land around Exeter, by the 9th Baron, which was subsequently increased with more in the north and south of the county.

In the 17th century the Clintons became linked by marriage to a notable West Country landowner – the Rolle family. George Rolle was a wealthy London merchant. In 1519 his family settled in Devon and his initial purchases of several small areas of land grew over the following few decades to become a considerable-sized estate. By 1883 his family had become the largest landowners in the county. At that time the Rolle Estate owned nearly 54,000 acres of Devon.

The Hon. Mark Rolle inherited the estate in 1852 and over the next half century set about improving his land holding. In 1907 the estate passed to Charles John Robert, the 21st Baron Clinton. As well as continuing with more developments and improvements to the Estate his passion and knowledge of trees led to a number of public appointments. The most notable was as Parliamentary Secretary to the Board of Agriculture. In 1919 he was a founder of the Forestry Commission and became its second chairman. So it is perhaps not surprising that the first two Forestry Commission plantations in England were planted in Devon. On his death at the age of 94 years, he was succeeded in 1965 by Gerard Fane Trefusis who became the 22nd Baron. Today the present Lord Clinton and his family continue to play an active part in the running of their estate which still includes the East Devon Pebblebed Heaths.

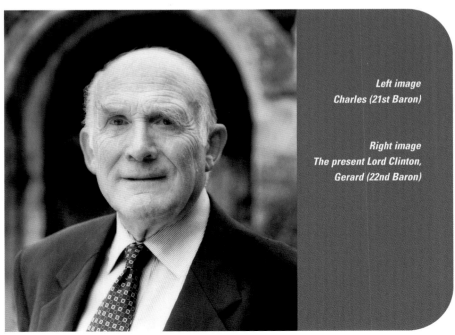

Left image
Charles (21st Baron)

Right image
The present Lord Clinton,
Gerard (22nd Baron)

social history

Over a thousand years ago during late Saxon and early Norman times, East Budleigh Common was part of the single royal manor of 'Budley'. For administrative purposes Devon was divided into 'Hundreds' and Budley was the biggest. It must have been a busy and important place. However, the reign of Henry I saw the first of several charters that carved up the land into five separate manors. Hayes Barton was the first to emerge. It came into the ownership of Bartholomew de Poer and his heirs for the next 200 years. Eventually the land passed with a sole surviving heiress to the Duke family, who finally leased it to the Raleigh family. It was here that Walter Raleigh was born and brought up. Despite many pleas by Walter, the Dukes refused to sell the title of the leased land and they set about reuniting the original royal manor into their ownership, as well as the greater part of Budley. The Duke dynasty only ended when three co-heiresses sold the property in 1676 into another great land-owning family – the Rolles.

The Clinton Devon Estates have owned the East Devon Commons for a considerable period of time: Woodbury since 1650; Bicton for almost as long; and Colaton Raleigh since 1786. Many of the lands have stories attached that cannot be substantiated, while a few are recorded in history. A former Second World War fighter pilot called Mutters once claimed his forefathers were smugglers and used to bury contraband on Mutters Moor. Consequently he attempted to prove he had some rights over the land. Not surprisingly his legal challenge came to nothing. The Mutters gang were certainly infamous during the 17th century and when one of the extended family became an agent of the government forces which were responsible for controlling and eradicating smugglers they murdered him. Parts of his dismembered body were thrown into bushes for passers-by to see. But there are other stories of more bloody confrontations with references to fights, Royalist skirmishes and even a fully fledged battle on Woodbury Common.

Hayes Barton,
East Budleigh. Birthplace
of Sir Walter Raleigh.

THE

booke of the common
prayer and admi-
niftracion of
the
Sacramentes, and other
rites and ceremonies of
the Churche : after the
vfe of the Churche
of England.

LONDINI IN OFFICINA
Edouardi Whitchurche.

Cum priuilegio ad imprimendum folum.

ANNO DO. 1549. *Menfe*
Martii.

Title page of the 1549 Prayer Book.

Image courtesy of D.P Miles.

rebellion

What is known is that after the death of Henry VIII in 1547, he was succeeded by his son Edward VI. These were troubled times. In January 1549 Parliament passed the Act of Uniformity enforcing the use of the Book of Common Prayer. This was a simplified form of service in English, instead of the old Latin Mass that people had practised for centuries. The Prayer Book was first used on Whitsunday, but the people of Stanford Courtney in Devon made their priest put on his usual vestments and say Latin Mass. This act of defiance soon spread. Within days Cornish parishioners were also demanding their Catholic Mass and a rebellion was born.

The Duke of Somerset sent Sir Peter Carew, appointed Sheriff of Devon in 1547, and his uncle Sir Gawen to deal with the Devonshire rebels. Their orders were to hold the area until Lord Russell could muster a sufficient force to quell the uprising. However, the Carews represented everything against which the people had risen. They were gentry who had profited from the spoils of the Catholic Church with everything to gain by forcing through the Protestant Reformation. Their interference perhaps inflamed the rebellion. The Carews were chased out of the neighbourhood, while the rebels imprisoned any gentry who were caught and proceeded to entrench themselves behind the little River Clyst, four miles east of Exeter.

By the end of June they were joined by Cornishmen and the combined forces closed in on Exeter, hoping that the city would join them. In early July the gates of the city were closed to some 2,000 Prayer Book rebels. Although they had many sympathisers within the walls, the mayor and corporation of Exeter refused to open the gates and a five-week siege began. Whilst the Earl of Bedford had arrived at Honiton, only fifteen miles east of Exeter, he dare not attack until the promised reinforcements of Italian and German troops arrived. It must have been the final humiliation for any government to use foreign mercenaries against its own countrymen.

Exeter could not hold out much longer. Its citizens were reduced to making bread out of bran that was normally fed to pigs. They were on the verge of surrender but the rebels could also not afford to wait. Reinforcements for the King's men could arrive at any time and so they decided to attack the troops near Honiton. A running battle ensued as the rebels first lost to clever tactics by the Earl, then gained ground again, only to be defeated when foreign reinforcements joined the fight.

August saw troops commanded by the Earl of Somerset leave Honiton and strike out along the ridge that runs south-west to Woodbury Common. The next day, they forced a passage across the river at Clyst St. Mary. The order was given to kill all rebel prisoners. In the fifth and final engagement the rebels were outmanoeuvred. Tragically, in the summer of 1549, Woodbury Common and the East Devon Pebblebed Heaths became a killing ground of its own people. It was by all accounts a terrible and bloody battle as the valour and stoutness of the rebels proved a formidable force. Lord Grey reported 'never in all the wars that he had been, did he know the like'.

The Prayer Book proclamation and seal placed in every English church in 1662.

Image courtesy of Exeter Cathedral.

home on the heath

In times gone by few people lived on heathland by choice. Well-drained soil meant that water was scarce and the poor soil was difficult to cultivate and unproductive. Dwellings were few and far between, often modest in size and their inhabitants poor. Indeed, even at the end of the 1800s some were so poor they were unable to afford any permanent home, living instead in a tent-like structure made from bent poles and covered in sacking. An elderly gypsy couple photographed in 1895 are shown scraping a living, perhaps from the sale of honey, as the man is weaving a straw bee skep.

Elderly gypsy couple scraping a living on heathland in 1895.

Image courtesy of Peter Kirby.

Photograph taken at Woodbury Camp by Edgar Leopold Layard in 1893.

Image courtesy of Fairlynch Museum.

Heathland has long been regarded as a sinister and threatening place. For most people used to living in a town or village, the idea that heathland could provide a home and livelihood has always been regarded with suspicion. From an outsider's view a heath was bleak, desolate and perhaps even dangerous. Anyone who dwelt in such a place was commonly regarded as living on the fringe of society, perhaps even an outcast or criminal. The notion of heath as being a twilight zone of respectable society was further propagated by its association with crime. The deeds of highwaymen and murderers did nothing to dispel the image. Constantly reinforced by popular writers from Shakespeare to Bronte, that perception lasted until surprisingly recently.

Life for people on heathland has always been hard. In the past it was probably not uncommon to see children collecting brush for the kitchen fire. At best heathland is marginal in value for farming but life became even tougher for heathland dwellers two hundred years ago. The rise of Parliamentary enclosure laws saw the fencing of large areas of common land and the people that lived there became largely dispossessed. Their plight went virtually unnoticed but a resurgence of interest in heathland came from an unlikely source. Artists and poets, seduced by its wild beauty, portrayed the wilderness with romantic verse and evocative paintings. Thomas Hardy and poet John Clare did much to champion the beauty of heathland.

inhabitants of heath

Throughout history people who inhabited heathland were considered to be at the bottom of the social order, living on marginal land that no one else wanted. At worst they were thought to be pagans. That perception is an ancient one, suggests Chris Howkins, a heathland expert. The Latin, Pagus, was used by Romans to describe a village or settlement, and its inhabitants were Pagani. The coming of Christianity to the western world saw the term Pagani used to describe those who were the last to be enlightened, living on remote heaths scattered across the European continent. It is thought that German and Scandinavian tribes associated these people closely with the heather amongst which they lived. In German the word for heath is die Heide, and the term die Heiden was used to mean pagan. So it is perhaps not surprising that we also get our English word for an unchristian savage – a 'heathen' – from the same root.

life on the commons

personal memories of a farmer and a soldier

Dalditch farm today.

the farmer

Philip Pigeon's parents moved to Dalditch Farm during the Second World War as tenant farmers of Clinton Devon Estates. Philip's grandfather had been the baker in East Budleigh. In the early 1900s, during his grandfather's childhood, it was quite common for children to take cattle up onto the heaths in the summer months and stay with them to prevent the herd wandering.

The early 1940s brought new opportunities to Dalditch Farm. The recently established Royal Marine camp nearby needed latrines emptied and ploughed into the surrounding fields. Although it was a traditional mixed farm with a small dairy herd, it was the chicken and egg production that did best. Milk deliveries started at 5am and the demand for eggs at the military camp was good. The arrival of the Americans in the lead-up to the D-Day landings brought much-needed supplies to the area. The GIs were friendly and fun. Fresh eggs and chickens were much sought after and payment was supplemented with valued extra rations of chocolate, tinned food and fuel. Not surprisingly farm-brewed cider proved very popular with the troops. Indeed, so good was the trade that Philip's parents eventually made enough additional income to buy a new, bright orange Fordson Standard tractor. During wartime, even in rural Devon, life was eventful and not without risk. The construction of a well-lit decoy airport on the heaths meant that German bombers were lured away from Exeter but came closer to Dalditch Farm. However, most of the family's wartime memories were not so perilous. Early one morning Philip's mother heard a commotion in the chicken run. Fearing a fox was raiding her precious hens she was surprised to discover an American GI helping himself to fresh eggs. Locking the chicken house door she ran to get reinforcements!

Philip was born just after the war. As a boy, he used to play on the heaths exploring the old wartime buildings with their overgrown flower beds. The construction of the new Exeter bypass saw the arrival of big bulldozers. They cleared much of the remaining structures to use as hard core for the new road. More peaceful were the hours spent horse-riding over the heaths. Summer used to see a few gypsy families arrive in horse-drawn caravans. They coppiced hazel to make clothes pegs and indulged in some horse-dealing. More memorable were big fires on the heath in the late 1950s. The inferno that started near Kingston Farm and swept towards Woodbury jumped roads and destroyed mature trees. The blaze obviously left a vivid impression on a young boy. By the 1960s the farm had a 40-strong dairy herd as well as sheep, chickens, and turkeys at Christmas. However, that era ended in 1976 when Dalditch Farm was returned to estate management and Philip began employment as a tractor driver on other farms. He continued to work for Clinton Devon Estates for over 22 years and today is still involved in ground maintenance.

the soldier and nurseryman

Frank Farr is the fourth generation of his family born in East Budleigh. He is a familiar face in the village where he has lived and worked his entire life, apart from 1939–45 in the army. For over 70 years Frank has sold flowers, and his grandfather, along with two uncles, all worked for Clinton Devon Estates. Frank's father, Fred, became head gardener at Syon House, the home of a prominent and wealthy man in the community. The start of the First World War saw mounted troops and 1,200 yeomanry camping on the heaths. The sound of the firing range above Yettington and the rumble of gun carriages pulled by horses was the prelude to impressive cavalry manoeuvres. It was not long before Frank's father joined the Devon Regiment and went off to war.

The Royal Devon Yeomanry.

Frank was born in 1918, a world very different to today when horse-drawn wagons were the only traffic. They carried cut turf and gravel from the heaths, or sometimes piled high with thatching straw. At that time the streams flowing off the heath powered many water wheels. Even the little Budleigh Brook that flows through the village at one time powered three mills: at Washmoor, Hill Farm and Thorn Mill. One mill always seemed to have chickens and piglets running around outside, and in the winter snow Frank fondly remembers it as being 'pretty as a picture.'

The old reservoir up on the edge of the heaths was a favourite place to visit, with trout rising on a summer's evening. Other places on the heaths were not so attractive – the old rubbish tip was an eyesore. But there were more popular parts where people gathered on windy days. During the 1920s and early 1930s kite-flying was a serious competitive sport. Inevitably there were other distractions for young boys. For as long as Frank can remember he had a pet ferret in his pocket. Rabbits were everywhere in those days and it was nothing to catch 20 or more in a day and sell them for as much as 6d each.

As a youngster, Frank attended the village school. The highlight of Monday was the arrival of a surprisingly quiet steam-powered truck, carrying library books and other goods. After leaving school he was apprenticed to a nurseryman and occasionally employed by Lord Clinton, when he even met Winston Churchill. In 1939 Frank joined the army and later volunteered for special services. Trained to parachute and use high explosives his unit was visited by top brass. Leading them was Winston Churchill. He remembered young Frank and wished him well with his mission behind enemy lines. After formalities Frank was interrogated as to how he knew the Prime Minister!

heathland harvest

Heather – Three different plants, bell, ling and cross-leaved heath are usually all referred to as 'heather'. In the past they were cut and used as fodder for domestic animals or utilised as low-grade roofing thatch or a stuffing for mattresses. They were also used in the production of besoms, as a rich source of nectar for honey and the making of ale. Heather makes a yellow-brown dye, which can be tinted more olive in colour by boiling in an iron pot or with the addition of oak galls. Heather has important medicinal uses, mainly because of its antiseptic properties. It is especially valued for the treatment urinary tract and kidney problems.

Gorse – Once regarded as one of the most versatile and sought heathland crops, gorse was valued mainly for fuel and fodder. It also had other uses. Apart from cleaning chimneys, fencing and thatching material, its flowers were prized for its bright yellow dye. But it was as faggots for the fire that gorse was regularly cut using a Devon hook. They catch light easily and burn strongly, producing instant heat. So they were especially valued for kilns and widely used in homes before the advent of cheaper fuels over a century ago.

Bracken – Highly invasive and unpopular today, bracken was an important heathland plant. Used as bedding for livestock and people, it can be utilised as a compost as well as fuel for the fire. Although a popular packing material, its real value was revealed when burnt. Its ash is high in potash, a useful fertiliser and, in terms of economic value, an essential ingredient in soap and glass making.

Man travelling by horse and cart from Woodbury Castle 1906.

Image from Clinton Devon Estates archives.

farming

The thin layer of acidic soil covering heathland results in a shortage of rich vegetation. Such land is unsuitable for intensive farming. The East Devon heaths were probably extensively used for grazing by early farmers from late Neolithic times. Rough grazing by cattle or sheep is thought to have been the principal use of these heaths throughout historic times. At Stoffard Way medieval field markers are still evident, but it is only in the aftermath of an accidental fire that old field boundaries sometimes show up. A solitary granite gate post is one of the few remains of farming activity up on the heaths but no written records remain.

Below the pebblebeds lie Permian marls that, where exposed, can result in richer soils. This is best seen to the west of Woodbury Castle. Here, at the base of the escarpment, several fields are still used for grazing stock. Over the last few thousand years cattle, horses, donkeys, sheep, pigs, goats and, perhaps even geese and chickens, have all been let loose to forage. By the end of the Saxon period, commons were increasingly being incorporated into manorial holdings. The arrival of Norman barons continued this practice, although written reference in the Doomsday Survey of 1086 is scant. No doubt the survey concentrated on formal assets rather than on marginal, largely unproductive waste land.

A glimpse of the historic use of the heaths can also be gained from other records. According to Charles Vancouver in 1808, writing 'A general view of the agriculture of the county of Devon'. *'The encouragement held out by Lord Rolle to the peasantry in his neighbourhood, to settle and make improvements on the borders of Woodbury-common and its dependencies, with the healthy appearance of the fir and some deciduous trees in the clumps and plantations of that common, sufficiently denote its powers for improvement, which being disposed of in planting, enclosing, and proper management, are capable of contributing essentially to the enlargement of the national stock. The soil along and towards the heads of some of the hollows, is found of a much better staple than would be expected from an examination of the ridges and higher parts of these commons, and affords opportunities for immediately enclosing some large tracts for the purpose of pasturage and tillage.'* Today, the plantations across the heaths reflect the sites of fields subsequently enclosed in the early 19th century.

common rights

The term 'common land' is often used generally, to describe any land in public ownership to which everyone has access. This does not reflect the true situation in law. Land must now be legally registered as 'Common' to have the status of a common. Even then access is not necessarily unrestricted. It is a complex issue with many local variations. Commons pre-date parliament and even the monarchy. They are a legacy from the dim and distant past when land was not owned but wild. 'Rights of Common' can be traced back to Anglo-Saxon times. The manorial system appointed owners but the peasants kept some customary rights as commoners. Typically the most significant right was for pasture, in order to graze domestic stock. Turbary was the right to dig turf or peat. Other rights include collecting wood for fuel and fencing, as well as gorse. Some rights may even have extended to the taking of sand and gravel. In reality the practice is a system of land use based on the granting and exercise of specific rights to manage the land in a particular way. Most rights were originally attached to properties rather than individuals. The sale of common rights only became more widespread in modern times.

The Enclosure Acts in the 18th and early 19th centuries effectively ended many ancient rights, although some did survive in parts of the country. Indeed, it is now not uncommon for a 'common' to have no active commoners at all, but this does not stop the land from being a common. This is the situation on the East Devon Pebblebed Heaths.

Children collecting furze faggots on heathland.

Image courtesy of Dorset County Museum.

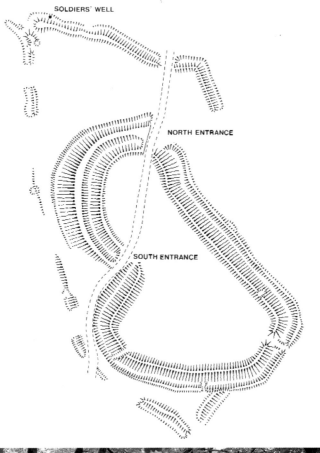

SOLDIERS' WELL

NORTH ENTRANCE

SOUTH ENTRANCE

settlement

Strange lumps in the landscape are evidence of the people that once inhabited the heaths. Throughout prehistory and especially since Bronze Age times people have attempted to eke out a living on higher ground. More importantly at the time, such places are strategically defendable. Thin well-drained soils are also easier to keep clear of trees. The heavily wooded richer soils of the valleys were dark and dangerous places, probably inhabited by wolves and bears.

Apart from Bronze Age barrows, the Iron Age hill fort on Woodbury Common and the foundations of 1940s military buildings, little evidence of permanent settlement on the heaths remain. In Hawkerland Valley the ruins of an old farm and a few village houses finally abandoned in the 1950s have also now all but disappeared. Only a few walls and an archway can still be seen.

Most heathland dwellers made a precarious living at best. Since Bronze Age times, when climate and soil conditions were perhaps more sympathetic to settlement, few people have actually lived on the heath. Subsistence farmers and gypsy travellers were probably the only people to be regularly seen. Elsewhere, little effort was made to colonise lowland heath until quite recent times. In nearby Dorset, and parts of South Devon, the area of wild lowland heath has been steadily eroded by domestic and industrial developments. As heathland gives way to housing in many parts of Britain, the national importance of the Pebblebeds grows day by day.

Woodbury Castle hill fort as it appears today.

Water fountain at Bicton Park which drew its water from the East Devon heaths.

water supply

As a county, Devon has a high rainfall, particularly to the west and over Dartmoor, where more than two metres a year is recorded. In contrast, rainfall over the Pebblebeds is low. Although records from Stoneyford reveal a variation, increasing from 666mm in the early 1990s to 1050mm by the year 2000, the average still amounts to only some 800mm a year. This compares to a national rainfall average of 920mm. On the East Devon heaths rainwater drains quickly, filtering down into the Pebblebeds and following the eastward slope of impervious clays. At Dotton the groundwater is reached by a number of boreholes where this water is pumped up to supply much of East Devon.

In the 19th century the building of a large ornamental fountain in the grounds of Bicton House, the seat of Lord Clinton, must have posed a challenge. Presumably water was also needed to supply the growing thirst of farms and houses on the estate. Such a water supply required the construction of a large underground reservoir on the heaths that tapped into vast amounts of water from underground streams. The subsequent construction first appeared on the Ordnance Survey map of 1907. By all accounts, the impressive, mainly underground building was big enough to house a large boat inside. A six-inch cast iron main carries the water to the gardens.

war and peace

The Pebblebed Heaths have a long history of military training since Napoleonic times and perhaps long before. Although there are only a few references to artillery practice prior to 1918, there is still evidence of many old structures surviving from the Second World War. For many years, the Royal Marines have had a permanent and famously challenging endurance course, as well as a grenade range on the Heaths.

The first modern-style military exercises on the heathlands were conducted by General Simcoe in the late 18th century. He was a former Lieutenant Governor of Canada and founder of York Town, better known today as Toronto. A fierce opponent of the slave trade, he returned to England as Commander in Chief, Western Defences. Based in Honiton at his Wolford seat, he set about recruiting a local militia to defend against the increasing threat from France. An experienced soldier he conducted large-scale military exercises with more than 200 pieces of artillery and, reputedly, thousands of horses. It was difficult enough to organise a fighting unit from untrained civilians, but it was the horses that apparently gave him the most grief. A long-running argument caused him to fall out with the largest local landowner, Lord Rolle. The issue was over who owned the horse dung on the heaths! General Simcoe thought Lord Rolle insubordinate and banned him from taking a military post if the French brought the war to England. The General was a battle-hardened commander, given the credit for saving Devon from the threat of invasion by Napoleon's army. The reason perhaps was because the sheer scale of his manoeuvres was so conspicuous, that even French spies must have been impressed. General Simcoe died in 1806 of an illness, after boarding a ship at Topsham, and was given a funeral fitting for a military hero.

Woodbury Common was used in the early 1900s as a First World War training camp not only for the Royal Devon Yeomanry, but also yeomanry from other south-west counties. Old postcards illustrate the life of the young men training for war and highlight the use of horse power over vehicles as used later in the Second World War.

War clouds again loomed over Britain during the summer of 1939. The mobilisation of armed forces and conscription of new recruits

Sir John Graves Simcoe.
Image courtesy of the archives of Ontario.

Royal Devon Yeomanry Camp near Woodbury 1905.
Image courtesy of Roger Stokes.

led to the establishment of a new training camp north of Exmouth. Rather fittingly the chosen site was on land owned by descendants of Sir Francis Drake. Construction of huts and buildings along with a small parade ground and access roads were all begun. Several hundred young men soon started their training for war on the adjacent Pebblebed Heaths. The ensuing recorded chaos paints a vivid picture as huts were built before the roads were even finished. The site was littered with pipes, cables, tractors, steamrollers and other construction equipment. Although the location was supposed to be secret, clues to its whereabouts in Britain were not too hard to guess. A recalled military pensioner, Corporal Thompson, described the scene for the newspapers: 'somewhere in the heart of the country on the banks of the River E, where the soil is red clay and a railway station lies nearby...'. As one later writer was to note, that probably fooled no-one, least of all the Germans. However, what would no doubt have confused any Nazi spy was the subsequent renaming of the railway station from Woodbury Road to Exton. The camp itself was then named after the next village, Lympstone, and as if that was not confusing enough, all the telephone numbers were listed as Topsham!

By 1940 the war had worsened. German forces had invaded all of nearby mainland Europe. The Navy had lost one of its largest battleships and Britain stood alone. The south coast of England was next in Hitler's sights. The year

Images below from the archives of the Royal Marines.

Below left – Rifle range, Bicton Common.

Middle – Mine sweeping training, Dalditch camp.

Right – Tarzan course, Dalditch camp.

Image on opposite page – Luftwaffe aerial photograph of Dalditch camp.
Image courtesy of Nigel J Clarke Publications.

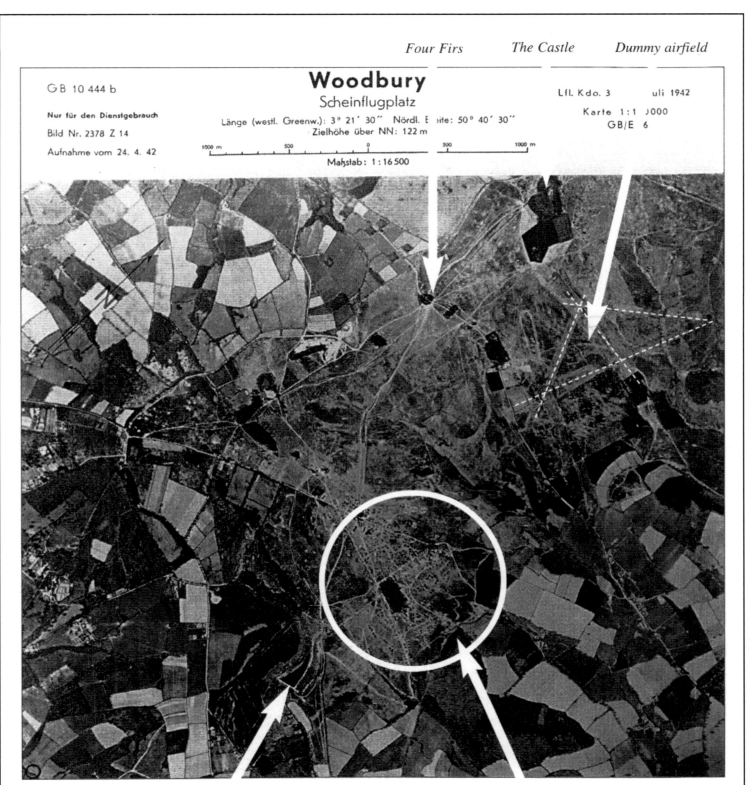

Four Firs   The Castle   Dummy airfield

GB 10 444 b

Woodbury

Scheinflugplatz

Lfl. Kdo. 3   uli 1942

Nur für den Dienstgebrauch

Bild Nr. 2378 Z 14

Länge (westl. Greenw.): 3° 21′ 30″ Nördl. Breite: 50° 40′ 30″

Karte 1:1)000
GB/E 6

Aufnahme vom 24. 4. 42

Zielhöhe über NN: 122 m

1000 m   500   0   500   1000 m

Maßstab : 1 : 16 500

Squabmoor reservoir   Dalditch Camp

began with the further conscription of an estimated two million young men and they would all need training. At that time it looked as though the heaths themselves would be under siege from our own troops. In 1941 the establishment of another camp, actually on the heaths at Dalditch instead of private farmland, began life under canvas. In contrast to the wooden buildings at Exton, the Dalditch construction mainly comprised of corrugated metal, semi-circular-roofed Nissen huts. It was built on a vast scale, so it is perhaps surprising that when government planners learnt of the War Office intention for the camp on the heaths, construction had already gone too far to move. The planners' main concern was that the heaths were the main water catchment for the local towns and villages. Considering the mistakes made in laying drains and subsequent legendary prevalence of stomach bugs among troops at the time, it is surprising the nearby civilian inhabitants in Budleigh Salterton survived the war!

Training soon increased to 800 men a month. At its height the Royal Marine Infantry Training Centre at Dalditch camp contained over 5,000 personnel. The escalation of military activity must have added considerable pressure to the surrounding heaths. Even before the arrival of American forces the scale of operations on the heathland was impressive. It substantially increased again

Parade ground, Dalditch camp,
East Budleigh Common.
Image courtesy of the Royal Marines.

Top left – Mine search training.

Top right – Royal Devon Yeomanry cap badge.
Image courtesy of Roger Stokes.

Below right – Pass out parade.

leading up to the allied invasion of German-occupied France. In 1946, just two years after the D-Day landings, Dalditch camp closed its barriers for the final time.

Over the centuries, through war and peace, the East Devon Pebblebed Heaths have seen their fair share of military action. The heaths have felt the feet of many invading armies – Roman, Saxon and Danes. They were probably even a training ground for the young Sir Walter Raleigh, playing childhood games close to his home at nearby Hayes Barton Farm. Through civil war skirmishes between Royalists and Parliamentarians, assembling militia during the Napoleonic campaign and battle practice through two world wars, the heaths have a long and distinguished tradition of military training for the defence of our country and kin.

woodbury castle

The Castle stands 175 metres above sea level, on a ridge of the Bunter Pebblebeds which consist of boulders and soft orange sand. This offers relatively dry conditions underfoot and, perhaps more importantly, it is easily excavated using a hand tool. While the present B3180 road runs through the castle today, the fort may have originally been built to control an ancient track on the same route.

Before the castle's first construction the surrounding lands would have looked very different. Tantalising finds of flints fashioned into implements suggest the area was used as a hunting ground by Stone Age people from around 9,000 years ago. But it was not until the first Neolithic farmers arrived three millennia later that the ancient wildwood began to be felled. The grassy clearings created were perhaps used to graze their domestic stock, or even attract deer for hunting. Many of these early people left little evidence of their passing but later arrivals did. During the Bronze Age, between 4,000 and 3,000 years ago, the appearance of significant burial mounds suggest a more highly developed culture. By now the surrounding landscape was largely denuded of forest, replaced by rolling grasslands and just a scattering of deciduous trees. Round barrows were built on this grazing land and two fine examples can be seen to the north of Woodbury Castle today. Another barrow to the south yielded a bronze dagger and stone battle axe during excavations.

Seen from the heights of Woodbury Common beneath a clear blue sky the scenery is nothing short of breathtaking. Overlooking the Exe Estuary to the west, the panorama stretches across the surrounding countryside and beyond to the sea in Lyme Bay. The strategic significance is not hard to imagine and Woodbury Castle is far older than its name suggests. It is a hill fort not a medieval castle and therefore of much more ancient origin. This strongly defended hilltop settlement probably also served as the stronghold of the chief who ruled the surrounding lands around 2,500 years ago.

The hill fort itself was constructed over several hundred years in different phases. Many of its impressive ramparts can still be seen today. Some appear to have been started and not completed, while the biggest and most impressive encloses an area of around 2 hectares (about 5 acres). During excavation evidence of a substantial timber palisade was found with perhaps a wooden tower over the main gate. Inside the walls a series of rectangular wooden buildings once stood, thought to have been built around 500 BC. Little is actually known of the lives of these people. Perhaps in response to new threats or an attempt to impress neighbouring tribes, construction continued. Shortly after the hillfort was completed the defences were once again strengthened. The inner ramparts were increased in height by about a metre and a new timber palisade added. Around the north entrance a new stone wall replaced the original timber posts. There is no doubt that Woodbury Castle was an important stronghold in its time. It must have been an imposing sight on the skyline with commanding views over the surrounding lands. So it is perhaps surprising that relatively few archaeological finds of pottery and other evidence of Iron Age life were discovered. The heyday of this particular fort seems to have mysteriously ended over three hundred years before the Roman invasion.

Image courtesy of Richard Austen

chapter 2

the present

heathland wildlife

AYLESBEARE COMMON

HARPFORD COMMON

HAWKERLAND

MUTTERS MOOR

COLATON RALEIGH COMMON

WOODBURY COMMON

BICTON COMMON

EAST BUDLEIGH COMMON

DALDITCH COMMON

Just what makes a heath can perhaps be found in the origin of the name: 'heath' is thought to come from Old English *hæd*, meaning open uncultivated land, and it is also associated with the word 'heather'. Effectively it is a place with few if any trees. Heathland is predominately a flat, open landscape where dwarf shrubs, usually heathers and gorse grow well.

The East Devon Pebblebed Heaths consist of seven separate Commons – Aylesbeare, Bicton, Colaton Raleigh, Dalditch, East Budleigh, Harpford and Woodbury. They lie on Triassic pebblebeds. Lowland heath is becoming rare in Britain and these Commons are recognised as sites of national and European importance. Over the last century, more than 70% of the East Devon Pebblebeds Heaths have been lost or destroyed. Clinton Devon Estates today own 80% of what remains and this represents the largest block of lowland heath in the county. Designated as a Site of Special Scientific Interest (SSSI) the area contains many rare plants and animals, and is particularly important for its birdlife.

Looking for all the world like moorland, heath can form at much lower altitudes. Heathlands generally have poor, acidic soils and low vegetation with rough grasses, gorse and heather. Most lowland heaths are man-made, not by design but by accident. They form in places once covered by deciduous woodland. After trees are felled the land loses most of its valuable mineral salts through weathering and becomes more acidic. The soil is no longer able to support its original woodland cover and heathland develops, although it does not always need people for its creation. On lowland heaths trees can be felled by gales and lightning can start fires.

The

The ins
wit

Th
p

42

The mesmerising heathland landscape at sunrise. The habitat is managed for biodiversity, achieving a rich and complex natural environment.

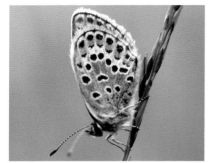

Some of the finest lowland heaths in Britain, rich in wildlife, can be found in South East Devon on the ancient Triassic pebblebeds. During the Triassic period it was a vast desert stretching into what is now France with colossal rivers depositing layer upon layer of pebbles. As the millennia passed the land overlying the pebblebeds became Ice Age tundra and when the climate finally warmed, thick forest. Around 2,500 years ago, Iron Age people arrived and built a great hill fort on one of its most prominent hills. Eventually all the trees were cleared and heath began to develop. Today Woodbury Castle overlooks some of the most important places for wildlife in Devon. Over time the heathland has become fragmented, but Woodbury Common remains the largest. The area consists of both wet and dry heath, lowland bog, pine and alder scrub with patches of deciduous woodland, all teeming with life.

The heaths overlie Triassic Bunter Pebblebeds, with some New Red Sandstone and Permian Marls, within an altitude range of 70 m to 150 m.

Insects

During the summer more than 30 species of butterfly are recorded most years. Silver-washed fritillary, brimstone, grayling, silver-studded blue and green hairstreak can all be found, as well as the emperor moth.

heathland wildlife

AYLESBEARE COMMON

HARPFORD COMMON

HAWKERLAND

COLATON RALEIGH COMMON

WOODBURY COMMON

MUTTERS MOOR

BICTON COMMON

EAST BUDLEIGH COMMON

DALDITCH COMMON

Just what makes a heath can perhaps be found in the origin of the name: 'heath' is thought to come from Old English *hæd*, meaning open uncultivated land, and it is also associated with the word 'heather'. Effectively it is a place with few if any trees. Heathland is predominately a flat, open landscape where dwarf shrubs, usually heathers and gorse grow well.

The East Devon Pebblebed Heaths consist of seven separate Commons – Aylesbeare, Bicton, Colaton Raleigh, Dalditch, East Budleigh, Harpford and Woodbury. They lie on Triassic pebblebeds. Lowland heath is becoming rare in Britain and these Commons are recognised as sites of national and European importance. Over the last century, more than 70% of the East Devon Pebblebeds Heaths have been lost or destroyed. Clinton Devon Estates today own 80% of what remains and this represents the largest block of lowland heath in the county. Designated as a Site of Special Scientific Interest (SSSI) the area contains many rare plants and animals, and is particularly important for its birdlife.

Looking for all the world like moorland, heath can form at much lower altitudes. Heathlands generally have poor, acidic soils and low vegetation with rough grasses, gorse and heather. Most lowland heaths are man-made, not by design but by accident. They form in places once covered by deciduous woodland. After trees are felled the land loses most of its valuable mineral salts through weathering and becomes more acidic. The soil is no longer able to support its original woodland cover and heathland develops, although it does not always need people for its creation. On lowland heaths trees can be felled by gales and lightning can start fires.

sinks over distant Dartmoor, a strange churring sound carries across the silent heath, followed by a wing clap or two. A nightjar has risen into the air from its daytime retreat. Its buoyant, floating flight, as it hovers and wheels against the afterglow of a setting sun is one of nature's most memorable sights. The white wing patches of the male flash as he cartwheels over the heath on falcon-like wings. Gradually his soft churring call may descend into a slow bubbling. Then he disappears from sight into a tree. The nightjar is unique among migrant British birds. They do not sit across a branch like all others, they sit along it and their camouflage is among the best on earth. Indeed, so good, that a nightjar crouching on the ground, eyes closed, surrounded by dead bracken and broken twigs, is almost impossible to distinguish, even from just a few paces away.

Over 70 breeding bird species have been recorded so far, notably nightjar *Caprimulgus europaeus*, hobby *Falco subbuteo* and Dartford warbler *Sylvia undata*.

Plants

The heaths contain three species of heather found in Britain – ling, bell and in the wetter areas, cross-leaved heath. Western gorse is common as is the European gorse with some patches of the larger Common gorse. The wet heath and boggy areas are of particular interest to botanists with a range of unusual plants such as pale butterwort, bog pimpernel, sundews, lesser butterfly orchid and saw-wort with many species of sphagnum moss.

The higher and drier areas are covered with heath dominated by heather *Calluna vulgaris*, bell heather *Erica cinerea*, western gorse *Ulex gallii*, bristle bent-grass *Agrostis curtisii* and purple moor-grass *Molinia caerulea*.

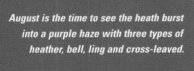

August is the time to see the heath burst into a purple haze with three types of heather, bell, ling and cross-leaved.

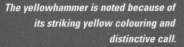

The yellowhammer is noted because of its striking yellow colouring and distinctive call.

Dartford warbler
The habitat provides a breeding ground for many birds including some rare species such as the Dartford warbler which favour the dense gorse.

Southern damselfly
The globally rare southern damselfly which can be found near shallow streams.

Nightjar
Rare summer visitor that nests on the ground. Flies at dawn and dusk to make best use of the light to hunt moths. Image courtesy of RSPB.

Dragonflies are also common, including the southern damselfly, a rare species in Britain that is confined to just a few parts of the south-west of England. Among the 21 breeding species recorded are the small red damselfly *Ceriagrion tenellum*, southern coenagrion *Coenagrion mercuriale* and the downy emerald damselfly *Cordulea aenea*.

The bog bush cricket *Metrioptera brachyptera* also has an important place in the food chain – the yellowhammer feeds its nestlings on young crickets.

Birds

Beneath the ramparts of Woodbury's Iron Age hill fort, the heathlands attract a good variety of birds. Stonechat, yellowhammer, curlew and tree pipit can all be seen or heard at various times in the year. The woodlands provide nesting for buzzard, kestrel, raven and green woodpecker. Even the hobby can be seen passing through on migration and may remain during the summer, attracted by the wealth of dragonflies. To watch this fast-flying falcon catch and consume a dragonfly while still in flight is thrilling to watch. So too is the rare view in winter of a hen harrier quartering the ground or great grey shrike perched on the branches of some scrub.

The East Devon Pebblebed Heaths are particularly famed for their population of Dartford warbler. This bird is more commonly found much further south. Feeding on insects year round may seem a tough task during a British winter but our increasingly mild climate has given them an opportunity. The East Devon heathlands were one of their original strongholds in Britain and they are still doing well.

Nothing can compare to a walk on a calm summer's evening when the busy birdlife of day gives way to the quiet of dusk. As the sun

Grasses and bracken *Pteridium aquilinum* are common in places, so too is bramble *Rubus fruticosus* and scrub with scattered pines *Pinus* and birches *Betula*.

A series of shallow valleys has allowed distinct changes of vegetation to develop. The dry heath gives way to wet heath with flushes on the valley sides, and to valley mire with patches of willow *Salix* scrub mainly on the valley floors. Here bell heather is replaced by cross-leaved heath *Erica tetralix* and characteristic species are common sedge *Carex nigra*, meadow thistle *Cirsium dissectum*, lousewort *Pedicularis sylvatica*, bogbean *Menyanthes trifoliata*, heath spotted orchid *Dactylorhiza maculata*, lesser butterfly orchid *Platanthera bifolia* and sharp-flowered rush *Juncus acutiflorus*. Other species associated with the wetter areas include bog asphodel *Narthecium ossifragum*, sundews *Drosera* spp., pale butterwort *Pinguicula lusitanica*, bog pimpernel *Anagallis tenella*, common cottongrass *Eriophorum angustifolium* and the club-moss *Lycopodiella inundata*. Mineral-rich flushes support tawny sedge *Carex hostiana*, carnation sedge *C. panicea*, bog rush *Schoenus nigricans* and devil's-bit scabious *Succisa pratensis*. Brown mosses can also be found here, such as *Sphagnum scorpioides*, *Campylium stellatum* and *Drepanocladus revolvens*.

Mammals and reptiles

The heathlands of East Devon are also good places to see wild reptiles and mammals. Adders live in the dry parts while grass snakes often frequent the wetter places as they hunt for frogs. Common lizards bask on the banks, warm stones and logs in spring and summer. The heath also supports a thriving population of roe deer.

Roe deer
The responsible management of wild deer is an integral part of heathland conservation.

Adder
Out of the six reptiles to be found in Britain, four can be found on the heaths including the adder.

Pale butterwort
Found in wet, boggy areas. These plants draw their nutrients from attracting insects onto their leaves which are then stuck and digested using an acid within the leaf.

stewards of the estate

In the past the person responsible for the smooth running of the Estate was variously known as a 'Steward' or 'Land Agent' and several have served the Rolle and Clinton Devon Estates over the last two centuries. Today the Estate is a large and complex modern business, yet many issues would undoubtedly have been familiar to its managers long ago. In the mid 1800s life may have moved a little slower but the work was not at all easy. Finding the right person for the job would have presented a challenge.

It was perhaps not until the publication of *The Book of the Landed Estate* by Robert Brown in 1869 that progressive landowners had a real guide to what makes a good land agent. It began with one year's practical work under a high-class farmer, experiencing all types of jobs. This would be followed by a year on another farm in a different county to broaden the experience, before attending agricultural college. After qualifying he should gain employment in the offices of a good land surveyor before seeking his first employment with a land agent on an estate where extensive improvements were being carried out.

Robert Hartley Lipscomb was the first of a new breed of land agent, serving from 1865 to 1892. He had most of the credentials for the job, having trained on farms and estates in the north of England and Scotland. He was well liked and respected in the local community and served the Estate for some 27 years. During that time he introduced many modern practices and embarked on a significant programme of building and development across the Estate including the construction of many cottages and 'model farmsteads'.

He contributed a series of articles to the monthly *Land Agent's Record* entitled 'Old Hints to Young Land Agents'. His writing was witty, lively and often shrewd. The articles also tell us something of his personality, a man who was happy in his work, and who wrote prolifically. Indeed volumes still contained in the Rolle Estate archive are thought to represent some 50,000 letters!

Robert Hartley Lipscomb
Steward to the Rolle Estate 1865–1892.

AYLESBEARE Common.

NOTICE is hereby given that the Burning into Ashes on this Common of Turf growing thereon, whether for Sale or not, is illegal, and that all persons thus destroying the Turf will be Prosecuted.

Also that the removal of Turf or Furze from off the Common for the purpose of burning it elsewhere into Ashes is illegal, and that all persons so acting will be prosecuted.

All persons, whether residing in or out of the Parish of Aylesbeare are warned against selling or buying such Turf or Ashes, and all persons entitled to rights of Common, are hereby invited to assist the Lords of the Manor (by giving information and otherwise) in their efforts to protect the Common from depredations.

BY ORDER of the Trustees of the Will of JOHN, LORD ROLLE, deceased, Lords of the Manor of Aylesbeare.

R. H. LIPSCOMB,
Steward.

East Budleigh, April 9, 1883.

19th-century notice and correspondence concerning the rights on the Commons.

With such a demanding, and at times very stressful, job it is remarkable how much time Lipscomb spent on 'Commons' business. The Estate archives have many letters and documents concerning the management of common land and supporting those with rights of common. Lipscomb was passionate about preserving the 'herbage and turf of the Commons' for the benefit of the Commoners and their children. In 1888 he was instrumental in setting up a 'Commoners Rights Protection Committee'. He erected notices, chaired meetings in a personal capacity as well as 'Agent' of the Estate. Lipscomb gathered evidence and prosecuted outside parishioners who carried off or received the produce of the Commons. It is interesting to note the passion surrounding the Commons. A number of letters survive from individuals writing to Lipscomb with evidence of wrong-doing by others. In June 1890 Henry Coles from Halls Farm, Aylesbere wrote:

'In answer to your letter I went to Aylesbere Common and seen George Salter & he had not got any ashes but John Salter is burning a heap of turf to ashes in his Orchard plot close to the house…'

The amount of time and resources consumed by all this activity (for hardly any economic gain) is remarkable by any standard. It demonstrates the Estate's and Lipscomb's passion for (in his words):

'the inward knowledge that you can look the whole world in the face and say that you have done your duty, and something more than your duty.'

By all accounts Robert Lipscomb was a tough act to follow and is given due credit for setting the mould for the modern land agent.

The Honourable Mark Rolle also had a passion for supporting the Estate's Commons and their Commoners. In August 1888, whilst his Agent Lipscomb was setting up the Commoners Rights Protection Committee, Mark Rolle was supporting him by executing a deed of gift whereby land at Hayes and Knowle would be added to the Commons.

As Mark Rolle said:
'It will give me much satisfaction thus to meet the wishes of the Commoners in the matter.'

Subsequent Stewards and Agents of the Estate have found themselves drawn into the complex and colourful world of the Commons, exercising much energy in responding to evolving Commons legislation and the changing requirements of the time; as well as dealing with a whole range of 'goings on' and illegal activity, from arson to gypsy encampments.

Today, the latest 'Steward' of the Estate is John Varley. Appointed for his business experience, with a background in global telecommunications, rather than traditional training as a chartered surveyor, John has adapted to his new role, helped by appointments to the Board of the Countryside Agency and the Commission for Rural Communities.

Although focused on delivering commercial objectives, the role of 'Steward' (or Chief Executive) again encompasses setting and executing a strategy for the Estate's Commons. Interestingly, the launch of the Pebblebed Heaths Conservation Trust in 2007 in many ways mirrors Lipscomb's role in the formation of the Commoner's Rights Protection Committee in 1888.

The role of 'Steward' is undoubtedly just as demanding as any jet-setting career with a multinational company and perhaps far more fulfilling, as John is the first to admit.

'The satisfaction of seeing the work through from first thoughts to fruition is priceless, and one that I really enjoy. The East Devon Pebblebeds are highly valued, and popular with local people and visitors alike. Enhancing their wildlife and preserving their rich history is a real priority. If we can also make the heaths a prime example of good habitat and amenity management, it will contribute substantially to the quality of life for us all.'

Pebblebed Heaths
CONSERVATION TRUST

NOTICE.

Preservation of COMMONERS' RIGHTS.

PARISHES OF AYLESBEARE, BICTON, COLATON RALEIGH, EAST BUDLEIGH, HARPFORD, NEWTON POPPLEFORD, & WOODBURY.

At the request of a large number of the Commoners interested in the above named Parishes,

A MEETING

Of Householders and Occupiers in the said Parishes will be held on

THE COMMON,
AT
WOODBURY CASTLE,
ON
Wednesday next, 28th inst.,

At 4 o'clock in the Afternoon, to consider what steps shall be taken for the Protection of the Commoners' Rights,

(By Request,)

R. H. LIPSCOMB.

March 21st, 1888.

W. J. BARNS, Printer, Bookseller, and Stationer, Budleigh Salterton.

Notice inviting commoners to a meeting which would establish the Commoners Rights Protection Committee.

Bungy Williams MBE senior commons warden

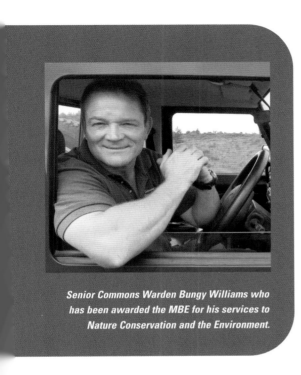

Just how a tough Royal Marine became a champion of heathland conservation is a surprising story. Today Mike (Bungy) Williams, is acknowledged as one of the most respected conservation practitioners of lowland heath management in the country. But it was not always so. Bungy is the first to admit that this was not a job he had ever imagined doing. Perhaps better described as a 'poacher turned gamekeeper' with a unique set of talents, the story of his conversion is as remarkable as the area he now manages.

A former Sergeant Major, physical training instructor, Bungy Williams proudly served with the Royal Marines for 24 years. Yet while travelling worldwide with the Commandos was an amazing experience, he could not wait to get back to his adopted home of Devon. Woodbury Common was an area he knew well from his warfare training days. After retiring from the service he took the opportunity to work with Clinton Devon Estates, who have a long history of military training on their land. After all, who better to interface with the Royal Marines than an ex-marine? Part of his new duties also involves lecturing recruits on the natural importance of the Pebblebeds. He seems to take particular perverse pleasure in informing them of the thousands of venomous adders lurking amongst the heather.

The turning point in his career arose from an unlikely friendship with Pete Gotham, a wildlife expert with a particular interest in birds. His easy-going lifestyle was as far removed from Bungy's military upbringing as can be imagined. 'Pete soon became my conservation guru', Bungy comments. A shared interest in local ales undoubtedly also helped.

When Bungy first started work with Clinton Devon Estates his job involved checking car parks, clearing rubbish, checking signage, footpaths and gates. With just a few hundred pounds, funding for winter scrub clearance there was no conservation management plan. All that changed when external funding arrived from the Countryside Stewardship Scheme. 'It was a big step forward', explained Bungy, 'today the work is much more complicated. From a day to day operation we now have a management strategy which extends over decades. And the new plans cover archaeology as well as scrub and bracken clearance.' Bungy learnt on the job. The next leap forward was the securing of Heritage Lottery funding and his work stepped up a gear. New machinery and vehicles today allow him to do in days what previously had taken months of back-breaking labour. There is now little waste to the operation as even the cleared scrub and timber is sold for chipping or fire wood. Driven by the economies of farming, the East Devon Pebblebed Heaths no longer have commoners interested in the land. Today, Bungy organises a 'flying herd' of cattle to graze certain areas.

Standing on the hillside below Woodbury Castle, Bungy's interest in natural history and pride in his work is obvious. His wide knowledge of the Pebblebeds comes from practical experience and a deep commitment that he is doing something really worthwhile and that he also happens to enjoy. His efforts were recognised in 2004 when he was awarded the MBE for Services to Nature Conservation and the Environment.

Pete Gotham retired RSPB warden

Pete Gotham – retired RSPB Warden.

Managing the wild and wind-swept heaths of East Devon demands many special skills. Pete Gotham originally worked as a quantity surveyor until a fascination with birds led him to a major career change. As a warden for the RSPB he helped manage some of their most famous reserves in the East of England, before being lured to Devon. For 18 years he was the Senior Warden for Aylesbeare Common and Exe Estuary, as well as RSPB Reserve Manager for Devon and Cornwall. Although the Pebblebeds are the fifth largest lowland heath in Britain outside of the New Forest, few people seem to think of Devon when it comes to heaths. Pete explained. 'Aylesbeare has always been a bit of a Cinderella reserve. The Pebblebeds are very underrated. They have lots of western gorse with Dartford warblers and nightjars, also some curlew and nesting snipe. Heathland is nutrient-poor and well drained so the plant life is a bit limited, but dry conditions can force flowers into bloom and then you can count over a million seed heads in a square metre. It's an amazing sight.'

The friendship between this bearded conservationist and the burley ex-Royal Marine, Bungy Williams, has undoubtedly benefited the management of the heaths. When Pete first arrived he inherited a sprayer and wheelbarrow chained to a post in the woods. Times have changed. Today the equipment is much more sophisticated. Bird life has improved dramatically. The sight of a hen harrier in winter is an occasional treat. Even the rare dormouse is doing well, taking advantage of the high number of nest boxes put up for birds.

Pete believes that if Clinton Devon Estates had not owned the Pebblebeds, much of the heath would have long since gone, fragmented and improved for farming. 'Luckily there have only been one or two major hiccups in its history. Thankfully, plans for a golf course many years ago never got permission. Since then the Estate has been very committed to the environment, as we can see by the wealth of rare birds on the heaths.'

John Wilding general manager of forestry

John Wilding – General Manager of Forestry.

As Forest Manager to the Clinton Devon Estates, John Wilding manages trees for commercial, environmental and social benefit. However, increasing the natural diversity of the woodlands as a by-product of that operation obviously gives him great pleasure.

Large areas of woodland surround and extend onto parts of the heaths. Most were planted but now natural regeneration is permitted in some places producing a mix of conifers and broadleaf trees along with more clearings. Many of the more mature trees date back to plantings in the early 1800s. The Estate records go back many centuries and the planting history of Hayes Wood, Uphams plantation and the trees around Woodbury Castle are well documented.

Outside the SSSI areas on the heaths there are still opportunities for enhancing the wildlife value of the woodlands and the heath itself. Nightjars profit from the clearing of conifers because replanting with young trees creates ideal nesting areas. And they are not the only birds to benefit. Crossbills feed mainly on pine seeds, deftly extracting them from cones using their curiously shaped bills.

Large parts of the woodlands are also open to public access, so any use for shooting and military training is strictly controlled. In the past dead wood was removed, but now it is only done for safety reasons near footpaths and access ways. Elsewhere it is left to rot and that provides food and shelter for many more wild animals and plants. John takes great pride in the fact that he is continuing a long tradition of woodland management on the Estate as the growing number of veteran and ancient trees testify. Some of them also have an historical value. A few of the older trees carry poignant scars – the names and initials of American GIs and British Marines in the 1940s, before they left for war.

A few old trees are outstanding. The Lone Pine on Aylesbeare Common has been dead for many years. During its long life it became a valuable marker for local boatmen offshore. Several years ago plans to fell it for safety reasons were shelved, after local witches threatened to curse anyone who touched the tree!

conservation

The majority of the East Devon Pebblebed Heaths are designated as a Site of Special Scientific Interest. Covering over a thousand hectares the area includes Aylesbeare and Harpford Commons, Bicton and East Budleigh Commons, Colaton Raleigh and Woodbury Commons and Venn Ottery Common. Although some are maintained as non-statutory nature reserves, the rest are all managed by their owner, Clinton Devon Estates in association with the Pebblebed Heaths Conservation Trust.

The wonderfully wild and open feel of lowland heath is well described in the definition of such places by the Devon Biodiversity Action Plan:

The expansive purple, golden and brown landscape which is lowland heathland is an evocative feature of southern England. Charged with history and alive with scent and colour, it combines an ancient origin with a vibrant living character. The power of heathland to evoke a sense of human desolation against the vastness of nature has led to it forming the backdrop to some of the most dramatic human stories of English literature over the last few hundred years.

Heathland is a product of human activity, formed where primeval forest was cleared for early agriculture on nutrient-poor soils, in the cool, moist climate of the Atlantic zone of north-western Europe. It relies upon the continuation of that human activity, and without it a reversion to woodland quickly takes place. However, while in the past heathland represented the most productive use which agricultural techniques could make of intrinsically poor quality land, today heathland survives only where there is a conscious intent to retain it, in the face of the capacity of modern agriculture and forestry to turn it to other uses.

Lowland heathland is defined as open uncultivated land below about 300 metres in altitude, dominated by dwarf shrubs – ling, cross-leaved heath and gorse – intermixed with acid grassland, bog, bracken, scrub and scattered trees.

The East Devon Pebblebed Heaths represent the largest block of lowland heath in Devon. In terms of its importance it is one of the top five sites in Britain and one of the largest contiguous heaths with no major roads transecting its Commons. It is a nationally important area and a good example of inland Atlantic-climate, lowland heath found in Britain and north-west Europe. One of its most significant features is the sheer diversity of animal and plant communities, which include 24 different kinds of dragonfly and damselfly. The southern damselfly is only known from 13 sites in Britain, two of which can be found on these heaths. The rarest butterflies found here include the pearl-bordered fritillary and silver-studded blue. Notable heathland birds for conservation purposes include the hobby, nightjar and Dartford warbler.

On paper the heaths are well protected. Not only are they a designated SSSI but also a Special Protection Area (SPA) and a Special Area of Conservation (SAC). The heaths are also within an Area of Outstanding Natural Beauty (AONB). The East Devon Pebblebed Heaths Conservation Trust works closely with Natural England, the Royal Society for the Protection of Birds and the Devon Wildlife Trust in an effort to manage the habitats in the best way possible to ensure the survival of the rarest species of plants and animals. The RSPB locally (on a peppercorn rent) leases two of the Commons as a Nature Reserve from Clinton Devon Estates.

In recent times the conservation of the heaths has moved up a gear, from simple day-to-day maintenance to proactive management, improving and even restoring habitats for certain key species. The award of a Heritage Lottery Grant offered a significant boost for a five-year enhanced conservation project. The creation of new heathland is not undertaken lightly as it requires considerable planning and even heavy equipment. More than 140 acres has been created since 1995 and a 40-acre former conifer plantation has also been restored to new heath. The removal of trees, clearing bracken and cutting gorse is all part of the routine annual work carried out by the management team. Open lowland heath is a rare habitat in Britain so the removal of trees and scrub is essential to maintain the nature of the habitat.

Heathland is on the retreat elsewhere in the country, so the natural value of the Pebblebeds increases every year. Careful management offers the opportunity to enhance the biological diversity and grazing is probably its most important tool. Today around 30 red ruby cattle are brought in to graze and trample selected areas. They are the Trust's secret weapon, helping to aid the recovery of the rare southern damselfly.

These heaths are a challenging place to manage because of their slopes and valley mires, but that adds interest and variety to the nature of the heath. Most English heaths are low-lying, giving few opportunities to see any distance. In contrast the Pebblebeds of East Devon offer rare views over heathland habitat. Everywhere you look, tantalising humps and bumps tell of past human activity over thousands of years. Here, there is a sense of permanency, where the remains of field boundaries and buildings lie half-hidden in the undergrowth. Hopefully, continuing careful conservation management will ensure the value of these heaths for people and wildlife for many years to come.

Careful conservation management is key to the successful biodiversity of the heathlands including grazing by red ruby cattle which helps to maintain the habitat.

EAST BUDLEIGH COMMON.

NOTICE IS HEREBY GIVEN

THAT THIS COMMON LAND HAS BEEN MADE SUBJECT BY REVOCABLE DEED TO THE PROVISIONS OF SECTION 193 OF THE **LAW OF PROPERTY ACT, 1925,** UNDER WHICH THE PUBLIC HAVE RIGHTS OF ACCESS TO THE COMMON FOR AIR AND EXERCISE. THE FOLLOWING ACTS, IF COMMITTED ON THE COMMON WITHOUT LAWFUL AUTHORITY FROM THE OWNER OF THE SOIL OR IN VIRTUE OF THE EXERCISE OF A RIGHT OF COMMON, ARE OFFENCES PUNISHABLE ON A SUMMARY CONVICTION BY A FINE NOT EXCEEDING FORTY SHILLINGS.

1. DRAWING OR DRIVING ANY CARRIAGE, CART, CAR, CARAVAN OR OTHER VEHICLE OTHERWISE THAN ON A PUBLIC CARRIAGE WAY.

2. CAMPING.

3. LIGHTING FIRES.

By Order

J. H. F. FOSTER,

Secretary,
The Clinton Devon Estates Company.

July, 1930.

"Journal" Printing Works, Exmouth.

recreation

The signing of a revocable deed in 1930 by Lord Clinton granted allowance for the general public to 'air and exercise' on the heaths. Although the East Devon Pebblebeds are known as 'Commons' there is only one property known to maintain legal rights of Common. This entitles the owner to graze either two horses and two cows or two horses and twelve sheep on Woodbury and Colaton Raleigh Commons. Since the signing of the original deed over 80 years ago, it is estimated that many millions of individual visits have been made by people during that time. Most seek to experience the peace and quiet of the heaths as a local amenity, enjoying its nature and splendid views, especially during the summer when coastal towns are thronged with holiday makers.

Implementation of the so-called 'CROW' Act (The Countryside and Rights of Way Act 2000) provided new opportunities to formalise the public use of the heaths. Effectively it would extend the public's right of access to the countryside whilst also safeguarding landowners and occupiers. The Act was designed to create a new statutory right of access and modernise the rights of way system, as well as giving greater protection to Sites of Special Scientific Interest. It also provided better management arrangements for Areas of Outstanding Natural Beauty and strengthened existing wildlife enforcement legislation. The Act provides the public with a right of access to mountain, moor, heath, down and registered common land specifically for the purposes of open-air recreation but excludes horse-riding, cycling, vehicles, organised games or any organised activity for commercial gain. However, transferring the East Devon Pebblebed Heaths to CROW permits the Estate to license restricted activities, such as horse-riding and cycling.

The heathland provides a diverse landscape not only for wildlife but also for leisure.

military training

The secret of any military success is the quality of training. The Royal Marines are no exception. For over 60 years the East Devon heathlands have contributed to the Commandos success. During the 1940s an infantry training centre was established by the Royal Marines at Dalditch. At its peak it contained over 5,000 personnel housed in 378 Nissen huts that could sleep 12 men. More than a hundred other huts were also used for administration, stores, drying rooms, medical quarters and workshops. Firing ranges, parade grounds and dry training areas all added to an impressively large facility. Today little remains to remind us of that once busy camp. Most of the buildings were demolished leaving behind just concrete foundations, some steps and brickwork bases. Scrub has now reinvaded and reclaimed the camp to such an extent that even from a short distance little evidence of its former military life can be seen. Like some lost civilisation the ruins are a reminder of another era, lost in a growing jungle of scrub.

The only buildings to remain include an elaborate wartime decoy lighting engine house once filled with generators. In the 1940s decoy lighting was used to lure German bombers away from the city of Exeter and airfield, towards a remote and unpopulated part of the heaths. Today they are put to more peaceful purpose, as a bat roost. There are also several concrete decontamination shelters now converted into bat hibernacula.

The Commando Training Centre at nearby Lympstone is now the sole training centre for the Royal Marines – both officers and marines. Active military training still continues on parts of the heath amongst the gorse and scrub. Its impact is more positive than one might expect in a number of ways. All recruits receive an induction highlighting the natural diversity and conservation importance of the heaths. More surprising was the result of a scientific study. Work on the status of the endangered silver-studded blue butterfly concluded that they did best wherever troops trained. The cutting of heather and gorse for camouflage inadvertently creates ideal conditions for the butterflies. It is an effective if rather irregular form of browsing.

Trampling by troops also appears to do a similar job to cattle, creating wetlands favoured by a rare damselfly. Even the digging of a simple trench and low bank to shelter troops, when backfilled, actually adds to the floral diversity of the hillsides. Perhaps literally more stunning is that some explosive battle training seems to

Today the heathland is used for modern military training exercises by the Royal Marines.

benefit a particularly rare bird. Colaton Raleigh Common near the grenade range has a disproportionate number of breeding Dartford warblers. While the attraction is not fully understood, it may be that regular disturbance keeps away predators and scavenging magpies from their nests. However, this successful tactic is not an option for the nearby nature reserves to use!

Perhaps one of the greatest benefits that military training has brought to the Pebblebed Heaths over so many years is the very presence of troops, unofficially policing the area. Dumping of waste and lighting fires is a major hazard on many lowland heaths elsewhere. As a deterrent to environmental vandalism the presence of armed troops seems to be a highly successful tactic. Also the willingness of Royal Marines to help fire fighters tackle a major incident once averted a much bigger disaster. The fire started when a model aircraft burst into flames. The quick response of Estate staff and Royal Marines as well as RSPB volunteers enabled the blaze to be brought safely under control. Maintaining a military presence on the heaths in the future is seen as a valuable asset to the management and security of the heaths.

quarrying

Much of our knowledge of the geology of the heaths has come from commercial excavations. The East Devon Pebblebeds form a distinct deposit generally around 20–30 metres thick of conglomerates and gravelly sandstones. They are of Lower Triassic age and underlain by Permian Marls, a material often rich in lime and clay. The beds change in character north of Uffculme where they are composed mainly of locally derived material, such as Devonian limestone and sandstone pebbles. To the south quartzite cobbles and boulders are much more common.

Blackhill Quarry is situated on Woodbury Common, seventeen miles due south of Uffculme, on the so-called Bunter Gravel Beds. Here the Pebblebeds form a deposit up to 31 metres thick of well-rounded pebbles which make up around 80% of the bed. The rest consists of coarse and fine gravel along with silt and sand. Not all the pebbles are pure quartzite. Some consist of other rocky material such as schorl, vein quartz, porphyries and occasionally sandstone. Sheets and small areas of plain sandstone also occur in the deposits. The beds at Blackhill Quarry were deposited by a complex of fairly straight, fast-flowing and relatively deep braided streams with gravel beds. Large amounts of gravel and silty sand was left on the downstream, lee side of sand bars in the rivers. The well-rounded nature of the cobbles and pebbles suggests the stones were deposited and eroded many times before finally collecting in the East Devon Pebblebeds. The quarry was first operated in the early 1930s by hand digging, sieving and breaking the pebbles with hand hammers to form road macadam. This was the practice in at least half a dozen locations on the Heath and many of these early diggings can still be seen. In 1934 new machinery was installed at Blackhill for the excavation and crushing of the quartzite which is thought to have produced

*The quarry pre-1960s and today the area
is being returned to heathland.*

the first bitumen-bound (tar) macadam in Devon. The quarry continued to work in a small way until 1953, when the Northcott Group of Quarries took over. Soon after this Blackhill became part of Western Quarry Sales Limited and subsequently EEC Quarries Limited, a subsidiary of English China Clays. On 1 June 1995 EEC Quarries became known as CAMAS Aggregates.

The macadam coated production has now been concentrated at the neighbouring Rockbeare Hill Quarry, while the present plant has increased its crushing capacity. Quartzite is a very hard and abrasive stone – it will even cut glass.

Two grades of sand are produced at Blackhill, a coarse one for concreting and a finer one for building purposes. Large ponds and pumps are necessary to feed the 60,000 gallons of clean water each hour to the plant and to remove the dirty water which contains up to 50 tonnes of silty clay waste each hour, back to the silt-collecting ponds. The quarry operation is planned to preserve the water flows of the Bunter gravel and also to leave natural slopes to common land.

The ready mixed concrete industry is the largest user of Blackhill's concrete aggregates and sands, although a large tonnage is supplied to builders and contractors direct. High-quality chippings for road surface dressing are supplied as far way as the Isle of Wight, Andover and West Sussex. The working areas at the quarry face are chosen in an attempt to harmonise with the surrounding area. When excavations end the workings will either be left as lakes or backfilled with silt and capped with overburden and landscaped, perhaps even becoming a focal point for amenity use. The intention is not to detract from the natural scenic beauty of the Pebblebeds and to realise any opportunities for public involvement with the heaths.

forestry

The thin acid soils of the Pebblebeds' higher ground is only suitable for the growth of shallow-rooted conifers and birch scrub. Trees naturalise more successfully on the lower slopes, where the soil is deeper and not so well drained.

Up until the Second World War the heaths were surprisingly bare of woods. Although Lady Rolle had the foresight to begin planting trees in the 19th century, her contribution was more aesthetic and designed to enhance the landscaping of the Estate rather than for commercial forestry.

Today most of the woodlands surrounding the heath are grown as a crop. Plantations of Corsican and some native Scots pine are used mainly for construction timber. Natural regeneration of native pine and birch is also permitted on some areas of the heaths, which increases their natural value. It is known that newly planted forestry is highly attractive to some rare birds. Nightjars particularly seem to home in on such ground between two and five years after planting.

The Estate's woodlands consist of 1,900 hectares in East and North Devon. Their commitment to forest management has resulted in 17% woodland cover compared with an average of 7% across England.

Once low-volume wood was harvested principally for the chipboard industry but needs have changed. Now woodchip burning for the Estate, as well as for domestic, industrial and commercial use is considered to be more sustainable, especially when woodchip is burnt to provide heating for innovative community schemes such as village halls. The heaths currently contain some 217 hectares (536 acres) of forested land.

Over time woodlands do change but the rotation of their habitat is long-term. Forest management can also mean different things to different people, as illustrated by one particular dilemma in the early 1990s. The mature Scots Pine on the Beacon (a tumulus) had reached the end of their natural life, so the parish council wanted to replace them. However, English Heritage would not allow replanting on the Beacon and English Nature was then charged with protecting the SSSI status of the heath and their plans did not allow for trees. A compromise solution was eventually reached when Clinton Devon Estates offered a suitable area on an adjacent redundant car park.

remarkable trees

Lovers Beech : Hayes Wood

The Lovers' Beech at East Budleigh is thought to be nearly 150 years old and has links to a very romantic story. Local legend maintains that Second World War soldiers, while stationed on Woodbury Common, carved the names of their loved ones in its trunk before embarking for France in 1944. The initials of sweethearts can certainly still be seen. However, trees tend to heal any wounds and as the tradition has long been continued, most of the carved tokens of love still visible today probably date from the 1950s onwards. So is Lover's Beech a poignant reminder of a link between American GIs and local life during the last world war? Well there may be some truth in the story. A few years ago, an elderly American gentleman reputedly met locals in the Sir Walter Raleigh pub in East Budleigh. He told them the story of his romance with a barmaid called Brenda when he was a young GI. They had sworn undying love to each other but he had not returned to England after the war. Over 50 years later he came back to retrace the steps of their evening walks through the woods to the Lover's Beech but their initials had sadly faded like their romance.

Lone Pine : Aylesbeare Common

Although long since dead, this famous local tree landmark still stands on a tumulus at a high point on Aylesbeare Common. In its prime it was used by fishermen off the nearby coast to help guide them safely into harbour. Several years ago there was a plan to fell the tree but on arrival, the tree cutters found a note attached to the trunk. It purported to be from the 'white witches of Aylesbeare' and warned that anyone cutting down the tree would be cursed. The lone pine still stands proudly, valued as much for the habitat it still provides for wildlife, as well as a local landmark.

Fire Beacon Hill

The clump of old pines growing on Fire Beacon Hill has been there for many years. It is the logo of Woodbury Parish Council and a much loved local landmark. In Britain Scots pine can grow to over 500 years old but many never reach that great age. The ones on Fire Beacon Hill are considered of such local prominence that the Clinton Devon Estates has brokered a compromise to continue the succession of the trees. By planting a new landscape clump in an adjoining car park it will not only ensure the succession of trees on this high point but also protect from future damage the Scheduled Ancient Monument and Site of Special Scientific Interest.

Cathedral of beech : Woodbury Castle

The Beech woodland on Woodbury Castle was planted in 1819. It now forms the major landmark on the heaths and can be seen from much of East Devon. The tall trunks and magnificent spreading crowns give a cathedral effect of pillars and buttressed ceiling. A walk beneath these mature beech trees high on the castle is very popular with locals and visitors alike.

Woodbury Castle from the air.

chapter 3

the future

east devon pebblebed heaths conservation trust

east devon pebblebed heaths conservation trust

The establishment of the East Devon Pebblebed Heaths Conservation Trust is a landmark in the history of the heaths and an important opportunity for their future. The gestation of the Trust in recent years is a result of changing attitudes over the last few decades. Nationally it was clear in the early 1980s that urgent action was needed to safeguard what remained of the nation's heathlands. Fragmented, degraded, vandalised and increasingly being sold for development, wild heath was under threat. Thankfully, many heaths already had a secure future in the ownership of organisations such as the National Trust, RSPB, county Wildlife Trusts and English Nature (now part of Natural England). But others did not. Even the way heaths should be managed was still being argued.

In 1981 the Wildlife and Countryside Act successfully reinforced the protection of heathlands already designated as Sites of Special Scientific Interest (SSSI). Subsequent European legislation has further enhanced that protection. In 1993 English Nature launched its Lowland Heath Programme, a strategy aimed at improving, restoring and even recreating former areas of heath. It was a bold move, just in time. Only a fraction of Britain's former heathland remained scattered across the country. In total the surviving lowland heath would hardly have covered the Isle of Wight.

Other landowners such as the Ministry of Defence, National Trust and Forestry Commission also hold considerable areas of heath. The plight of their wildlife and limited economic value have increased pressure to find the best way to manage them. The launch of the 'Tomorrow's Heathland Heritage' initiative in 1997 and more awareness of the issues affecting their future have resulted in major changes for the better.

Winter is the main season for heathland management work. The reason is that this avoids disturbance to nesting birds during the prime breeding periods of spring and summer. Reptiles, too, hibernate during the coldest months, so any ground work done at this time will be finished long before they emerge from their winter torpor.

Good management is the key to most successful outcomes and heathland is no exception. The decline and, in some places, the complete absence of traditional practices such as grazing and burning, has resulted in the rise of scrub. On the Pebblebeds of East Devon there are three other factors that also impact upon the health of the heath.

The boundary of Blackhill Quarry is adjacent to the SSSI but studies suggest that its workings have had a limited negative impact on the protected heath. Within the quarry there is inevitably some local noise and traffic disturbance during business. We must remember the area taken in as a quarry was a very unproductive heathland site, that bore the scars of a Second World War military camp and a thick dense conifer plantation. The SSSI, SPA and SAC will be enhanced by a better and more favourable wet and dry heath, being restored on the redundant areas, so as to join the main heaths when worked out.

Incredibly, restoration of worked-out areas of the quarry has resulted in the return of heath within its boundaries. Nightjar, Dartford warbler and silver-studded blue have all returned to breed. The future cessation of works may create an even greater opportunity for the new East Devon Pebblebed Heaths Conservation Trust to provide interpretation and information for public access to the heaths.

Public access to the heathland has increased since Lord Clinton's dedication in 1930 allowing a variety of activities for 'air and exercise'.

Royal Marine Commando training appears to have had a largely neutral impact on the nature of heathland and may even have enhanced it in places. Their presence deters off-road motorbikes and joy-riders, and military access tracks provide fire breaks, as well as bare ground for ants and beetles. Perhaps surprisingly, it seems that despite the disturbance of gun-fire and grenades, the increasing population of rare birds is a good indicator of no long-term damage.

Public access to the East Devon Commons has increased greatly since Lord Clinton's dedication in 1930, when people were allowed to enjoy fresh air and exercise. Since then the numbers of visitors walking, jogging, cycling and horse-riding while enjoying the fresh air, breathtaking views and wild surroundings have grown. Sadly the sheer weight of numbers is beginning to take its toll. Recreational activities are also much more diverse. We live in an increasingly crowded nation and access to the countryside for the greater population is now easier than at any time in history. The issues may be sensitive but the evidence unfortunately speaks for itself. Mountain bikes no longer seem confined to tracks, while lights and night orienteering disturb nocturnal creatures. The flying of model aircraft can disturb the tranquillity which is special to some people using the area. Horse-riding is beginning to erode well-used tracks and increasingly dogs are not being kept under control. In the days of General Simcoe and his militia training, horse droppings were a valuable source of manure worthy of a dispute. Today the issue is the quantity of horse and dog droppings being left along the most popular track ways. The resulting change in heathland nature is now becoming apparent. But other forces are also at work. Climate change is predicted to produce shorter, wetter winters and longer, drier summers. Heavy rain now appears to be exacerbating localised erosion caused by horses and bikes.

Controlled burning is an effective tool for heaths and is known as 'swailing'. Late February through early March is peak time for the use of fire. Completing all works by the end of March reduces the impact on wild animals and plants as well as on people enjoying the start of warmer weather. However climate change with an earlier onset of spring, may well affect the way that work is done in the future.

The physical management of the heaths in recent years seems to have worked wonders, resulting in dramatic improvements to the quality of the habitat. Traditional practices of burning, grazing and gorse coppicing, along with scrub clearance, pine removal, bracken control, firebreak bulldozing and subsequent mowing have all proved their value. Summer grazing on Hawkerland and Colaton Raleigh Commons has successfully controlled tussocks of invasive purple moor grass. While many areas are responding well to the new regime, others are more difficult. Bramble and scrub are still encroaching in some places and further management will be needed to maintain the plants and animals of the heath. The future looks good for the Pebblebed Heaths. The impact of climate change will be felt hardest where wildlife is constrained within small areas, so the contiguous nature of the heaths adds significantly to their chances of survival. Ironically, if given the chance, heaths are well placed to prosper in the future with wildlife already adapted to living on dry, well-drained land.

The formation of the Trust will provide new opportunities for funding the future of the heaths, plan for the succession of its management and increase its sustainability. As a charitable body it will help to engage with the local

community. Set up with conservation objectives approved by interested parties, Clinton Devon Estates has effectively agreed to increase public involvement with the the heaths. In the past funding was also sought to manage the archaeological sites for the benefit of public interest. It met with little success. A trust may be more eligible for grant aid. In 2007 the Trust became one of the first beneficiaries of the government's flagship Higher Level Stewardship Scheme.

The Trust aims to make its workings as transparent as possible, increasing community involvement and educational opportunities, and improving the quality of information to enhance the visitor experience on the heaths. The appointment of trustees with conservation and estate experience, historical interest and visitor management skills, will add to the strength, commitment and effectiveness of its performance. The Trust aims to work particularly closely with Natural England, developing a clear vision for its future to gain better recognition for the East Devon Pebblebeds nationally and internationally for its wildlife, geology and history.

Raising the status of the heaths is only a part of the plan. Clinton Devon Estates believe there is no point in raising the profile of the area without becoming an exemplar of best practice, whether as a modern estate or a heathland. Ultimately the Trust aspires to promote responsible use and appreciation of the Pebblebed Heaths as a national treasure for both wildlife and people.

Enjoying the natural beauty and wonderful views from the ancient ramparts of Woodbury Castle, surrounded by the history of so many human lives, is a humbling experience. Few places in Britain can tell such an epic story from just a single stone, spanning 250 millions years with monsters and mass extinctions, wars and rare wildlife, yet a very special pebble can.

Image courtesy of Richard Edmonds
Dorset and Devon County Councils.

Heathland is a fragile habitat easily destroyed or degraded, wiping out centuries of human history and rare wildlife. Yet in this place of such exquisite natural beauty, with breathtaking views and abundant fresh air, so many people still seem to take public access for granted. If we are to preserve such areas for future generations to enjoy, as we have done in the past, local communities must engage and value their use.

The national importance of the East Devon Pebblebeds for wildlife and people cannot be denied. Both Clinton Devon Estates and the East Devon Pebblebed Heaths Conservation Trust are committed to raising the awareness of their value by working with schools and local communities. But perhaps everyone who enjoys the peace and fresh air of the heaths should ask themselves, 'what can we do to help?'

If you are interested in ensuring a positive future for this special place, please contact or visit:

www.pebblebedheaths.org.uk

80

acknowledgements

The East Devon Pebblebed Heaths Conservation Trust would like to acknowledge the following people and organisations in helping to provide the valuable information and images within this book.

Tim Badman BSc Dip, Environment Group Manager, Dorset County Council
Professor Denys Brunsden OBE DSc (Hons) BSc, PhD, FKC, Jurassic Coast Trust
Professor Michael J. Benton FGS, FLS, Dept of Earth Sciences, University of Bristol
Julian Calverly, Photographer
Paul Clayden, Photographer, Image FX
David Daniel, Otter Valley Association
Richard Edmonds, BSc Earth Science Manager, Jurassic Coast World Heritage Site
Pete Gotham, retired RSPB Warden
Professor Malcolm Hart BSc, PhD, DSc, FGS, CGeol, CSci, School of Earth, Ocean & Environmental Sciences, University of Plymouth
Claudia Hildebrandt MSc, Assistant Curator of Geology, Royal Albert Memorial Museum, Exeter
Jon Lewis, Coastal Publishing
Matt Low, Conservation Officer, Natural England, Cornwall, Devon & Isles of Scilly
Roger Stokes

Organisations

The Clinton and Rolle Estate archives
Commando Training Centre, Royal Marines, Lympstone
Dorset County Museum
Exeter Cathedral
Fairlynch Museum, Budleigh Salterton
The Jurassic Coast Trust

index

Pebblebed Heaths
CONSERVATION TRUST

The history of the East Devon Pebblebed Heaths spans back over 240 million years from the beginning of the Mesozoic period including the Triassic, Jurassic and Cretaceaous periods, through the Tertiary and to the present day, the Quaternary period. Over its 240 million years of history, mankind's stewardship of the Pebblebed Heaths covers only a few thousand years.

The establishment of the East Devon Pebblebed Heaths Conservation Trust is a landmark in the history of the heaths and an important opportunity for their future. The Trust has been established to ensure that a sustainable plan is put in place to safeguard the future of the Pebblebed Heaths.

To date responsible management has resulted in dramatic heathland improvement with the return of many rare wildlife species including the nightjar, Dartford warbler and silver-studded blue butterfly to name but a few. The heathland is located in an Area of Outstanding Natural Beauty (AONB) and has been recognised by both UK and European designations including a Site of Special Scientific Interest (SSSI), Special Protection Area (SPA) and a Special Area of Conservation (SAC).

If you are interested in ensuring a positive future for this special place, please contact or visit
www.pebblebedheaths.org.uk

Triassic Period (250 - 200 million years ago)

East Devon lay within an arid centre of the super-continent Pangaea.
A dramatic change in climate occurred and vast rivers flowed through the hot desert landscape depositing thick layers of pebbles and sand. These pebbles help to form the East Devon Pebblebed Heaths today.

Evolution of Triassic Life
A critical period of animal evolution. The four legged animals of today evolved from the living groups of this period including frogs, turtles and crocodiles. The East Devon Pebblebed Heaths was home to the Rhynchosaur, a skeleton of which was found in 1990. This helped to confirm the East Devon coast which forms part the World Heritage Site as the richest mid-Triassic fossil site in Britain.

Jurassic Period (200 - 140 million years ago)

As Pangaea started to break apart and the Americas drifted away from Europe, sea levels rose flooding the Triassic deserts. The Earth's climate was relatively warm with very few polar ice caps providing ideal conditions for evolving life including dinosaurs.

Explosion of Jurassic Life
As sea levels rose they created deep seas and coastal swamps enabling an explosion of marine life. Many animals rapidly evolved and flourished taking advantage of the new habitat including reptiles and ammonites, which are related to the modern squid.

Cretaceous Period (140 - 65 million years ago)

A recognisable ocean appeared as the Americas continued to drift away from Europe. Mid-way through the period earth movements deep beneath south-west England tilted the rocks to the east. Both the oldest rocks - including the Triassic pebbles of the Pebblebed Heaths - and and some of the youngest rocks can be found on the East Devon World Heritage Site.

A Period of Extinction
The landscape became more hospitable where the first flowering plants evolved and the largest and most fearsome dinosaurs roamed the earth. All this was to change at the end of the Cretaceous period as a mass extinction took place and dinosaurs, marine reptiles and ammonites became extinct.

Tertiary Period (65 - 1.8 million years ago)

The Tertiary period marked the world as we know it today - one dominated by mammals.

Landscape Changes
The Tertiary period saw many changes in the formation of the landscape including the building of mountains known as the Alpine Orogeny, which affected the Devon area by causing land uplift. This can be seen by the southwards tipping of the rivers in East Devon including the tributaries which run off the heaths into the River Otter.

Over the last two m
landscape we have

Early Settlers...

Stone Age
Flint found on the hea
sharp implements indi
ground over 9,000 yea

To the present day

18th century
The heathland has pro
ground for military tra
General Simcoe - who
saving Devon from th
army - used the heath
including artillery and t
also used for training
continues to be used

million years in the making

...illion years the climate of Britain has varied tremendously with both warm and glacial periods - known as the Ice Age - which has helped to form the ...today. As the land became more habitable human intervention increased on the heaths.

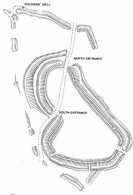

...s which have been fashioned into ...ate the area was used as a hunting ...rs ago.

Iron Age
The remains of a prehistoric hill fort, dated around 500-300 BC, can still be seen at Woodbury Castle. This scheduled ancient monument was probably used as a stronghold by the local chieftains. Sited on Woodbury Common, the castle has extensive views over the surrounding heathland.

Bronze Age
Early farmers began to clear wildwood in the area with bronze axe heads which opened the way for the formation of the heathland and the wildlife including plants and animals which followed.

...vided an excellent training ...ing. In the 18th century ... has been credited with ... invasion by Napoleon's ...s for extensive training ...ousands of horses. It was ... WW1, WW2 and ...oday.

19th century
The Honourable Mark Rolle - a notable local landowner - set about improving the area and his passion for trees can still be seen in the many mature plantations on the heaths which continue to be managed today by Clinton Devon Estates.

20th century
Proactive management of the heathlands helps to improve and restore the habitat. It is recognised by both UK and European designations including a Site of Special Scientific Interest (SSSI), Special Protection Area (SPA) and a Special Area of Conservation (SAC).

21st century
Today the heathland is protected by the East Devon Pebblebed Heaths Conservation Trust, ensuring the area is managed as a sustainable and bio-diverse landscape for future generations to enjoy. This has allowed many plant and animal species, some of which are rare, including the nightjar, Dartford warbler, silver-studded blue butterfly and southern damselfly, to live on the heaths.